THE AMERICAN SHORT STORY

THE AMERICAN SHORT STORY

A Study of the Influence of Locality in its Development

BY

ELIAS LIEBERMAN, Ph.D.

"Take civilization from this soil and there will remain to the inhabitants only war, the chase, gluttony, drunkenness. Smiling love, sweet poetic dreams, art, refined and nimble thought, are for the happy shores of the Mediterranean. Here the barbarian, ill housed in his mud hovel, who hears the rain pattering whole days among the oak-leaves—what dreams can he have, gazing upon his mud pools and his sombre sky?"
—TAINE in *English Literature*.

AMS PRESS, INC.
NEW YORK

Reprinted from the edition of 1912, Ridgewood
First AMS EDITION published 1970
Manufactured in the United States of America

International Standard Book Number: 0-404-03986-3

Library of Congress Catalog Card Number: 71-128995

AMS PRESS, INC.
NEW YORK, N.Y. 10003

TO MY MOTHER

FOREWORD

A FEW years ago the expectant critic used to scan
the horizon for the coming of the "American
novel," in whose pages the wonder of our new
nationality was to find a worthy elucidation. From
that moment of achieved national consciousness our
real literature was to begin. Somehow the ar-
rival of the book seems to be deferred, and our
critics are less sanguine in their prophecies about
it. In so far as they try for larger interpretation
of our national spirit, our writers of fiction still
fail in certainty and definite aim, and commonly
fall into conventionality or jingoism. American
fiction at its best is mainly an affair of localities.
It is the story of New England or Louisiana, of the
corn lands of Dakota, or the mining towns of the
Sierras, or the snows of Alaska, or, it may be, of
the crowded realism of the manifold life of New
York City. From it all we receive a succession
of vivid cross-sections of the life of particular localities. Consciously or unconsciously, therefore,
American fiction has taken the form of special
studies of the reaction between individual character and local environment.

This interest of locality has made the decisive

opportunity of the short story, which, as a literary type, with its characteristic emphasis upon "situation," is thus far the distinctive contribution of America to literature. Perhaps, after the host of short-story tellers have searched out the secret of every hamlet and byway, there may come those who, on a larger canvas may attempt weightier things successfully. Perhaps so; but they will certainly not neglect the harvest of their predecessors; and it must be emphasized that we no longer consider the short story as a primary school to the novel, or its writer as a novelist in knickerbockers. The short story has a being and an end in itself, and its independent future is safe.

Dr. Lieberman has hit precisely upon the study of locality in its influence upon the American short story for the theme of his valuable study. Undeterred by the vastness of the material to be explored, he has brought enthusiasm and sound method to the analysis of the precise debt, which, in a judiciously chosen series of representative instances, the American short story owes to locality. Himself a writer of short stories, as well as a student of literature in the better sense, Dr. Lieberman has known how to give his treatment both practical worth and readability. Writers of what Dr. Lieberman calls the "local short story" will find their aims and some of their specific problems defined more significantly than in any existing study of this precise subject. It is a singular

fact that the short story, in spite of its immense
extension, has so far attracted few serious students.
Readers of the short story—and who of us is not—
will find in the book an interpretation of certain
elements of American literary tendency that cannot fail to be suggestive. The work will be of
much value therefore as a work of reference for
the general reader as well as for the special student.

ARCHIBALD L. BOUTON.

New York University,
   Department of English.
      April 2, 1912.

INTRODUCTION

NEVER before in the history of our literature has there been so great a demand for fiction. The general literacy of our people through a system of free education has created a great reading public. Whether the cause of the demand for fiction on their part is a desire to escape from the humdrum cares of life, or a tendency to follow an intellectual line of least resistance, or an effort to batten an imagination starved by a narrow industrialism or commercialism, the fact remains that works of fiction are a very desirable commodity.

The fiction worker, the author, who meets this call for his wares is constantly searching for new material. The public is ever hungry and he must ever feed. His stock-in-trade must be constantly replenished. He draws from his own experiences mainly, if he wishes the stories he writes to be life-like and true. Seldom does he stray far afield because he feels that he can not give his work the convincing touches it needs without a profound first hand knowledge of his subject matter.

Thus in our novels and in our short stories we get a great deal of what is called "local color." A story is given a unique setting, let us say in

the slums of New York, in the West of '49, in
a New England village or on a Southern plantation. In each case the author reconstructs the
section for us as he has seen it. His setting
becomes a vital part of his story: through
demand for consistency it shapes to its own measure
his situations, his characters, his moral problems,
his pathos and his humor.

It is the purpose of this book to investigate the
influence which our numerous localities have had
on the development of our short story. I purpose to do this by taking up typical sections and
showing how they have been treated by various
short-story writers, what aspects of the localities
they have presented, what features they have emphasized and, in general, what influence the localities have exerted upon their short-story work.

In the nature of the case my treatment can not
be exhaustive. There are so many sections and
so many writers for each that it would be an impossible task to take up the work of each author
intensively. Even if done, it would be confusing.
I have limited myself to the following sections
as being fairly representative of our American life:
New England; the Mississippi valley; the lumber section of Michigan; Louisiana; Virginia;
Georgia; Tennessee; Kentucky; the far West; New
York City, with its numerous races and classes;
and Alaska. From the fictional use of these localities the reader can get some notion of the pos-

sibilities in territory not included. The task of being comprehensive is all the more difficult because within the last ten years almost every available claim to an interesting locality or a subdivision of it has already been made. From the Chinese quarter of San Francisco, the lumber camp of the North, the Jewish quarter of New York and the log cabins of field-workers in the South, themes for short stories have been evolved. Every point of the compass has a jealous and aggressive group of literary folk standing guard over it and claiming it as their own.

In the expression "American Short Story" in the title, I have included only work with a setting in the United States and by writers either native to the United States or long resident in it. Stories with settings in our Island possessions or in the various Central American and South American Republics have not been considered.

It is hoped that the student of American literature will find in this investigation a not unworthy contribution to the bibliography of criticism dealing with an art-form almost distinctively American. For the student and the writer of the short story it should prove a valuable résumé and should hint at the lines along which their own localities may be treated. Even the general reader ought to find the critical treatment of master short-story writers, an incentive toward a judicial selection of reading matter.

I have tried as far as possible to avoid critical citations concerning short-story writers from other sources. In almost all cases, I have quoted from the writers themselves and have thus given the basis for any conclusions I might have reached concerning the writer under discussion. These selections have been culled with great care and are, I trust, fairly representative of the point of view of the literary men and women whom I have treated.

For Chapters I and II no special originality is claimed except in the disposition of the subject matter. They are introduced to refresh the reader's mind concerning the entire subject and to give a philosophical basis for a study of locality in its influence upon the American short story.

With a realizing sense of its shortcomings and yet with a feeling that it fills a little niche all its own in impressionistic literary criticism of the short story, this work is presented to the reader.

TABLE OF CONTENTS

THE AMERICAN SHORT STORY

CHAPTER I

ALL fiction has its basis in reality. It is the product of the constructive imagination putting together old material into new combinations. Even in such flights of fancy as the pseudo-scientific romances of Edgar Allan Poe, Jules Verne and H. G. Wells there is a substratum of fact. The note of reality must be struck even in fiction to distinguish the product of the fiction worker from the unrelated maunderings of the insane. It follows, therefore, that the laws of human character and their processes of action, reaction and interaction obtain in fiction as they do in the living world about us.

Men and women, the raw material of nearly all stories, are subject, through the agency of their environment, to decided modifications in their points of view, customs and habits of thinking and acting.

1

It is psychologically true that we are the products of heredity and environment. Thousands of influences, like so many currents in a great bay, cross and recross, each one modifying, though sometimes imperceptibly, the character of a man. Out of the raw material of his nativity there is shaped for good or for evil the complex character of the modern human being. His joys, his sorrows, his struggles, —all leave their impress. On the vast stage of the world amidst the unceasing dins of the life drama, the individual actor shows all his heroic strength and all his pitiful weakness. Sometimes he is a god battling against great odds; sometimes mere driftwood borne downstream. But ever, as he lives and toils, nature and his fellow man set and reset his characteristics into kaleidoscopic combinations.

Let us examine some of the most important forces that determine localities and therefore types of men and women. When a community finds itself isolated from others there is a tendency to continue the same habits and customs generation after generation. In the "Legend of Sleepy Hollow" Washington Irving, picturing the seclusion of the place and its effect on the inhabitants, relates how old customs were perpetuated and innovations frowned upon. Everyone conformed to previous traditions so that time went on without making changes until there was one hundred years' difference between Sleepy Hollow and other communities.

Marken in Holland is an interesting example of what isolation can do. The European tourist, after having "done" the famous art galleries at Amsterdam is induced to go to Marken. There, he is told, he will see the fisher-folk in the dress of centuries back. In the streets of Amsterdam the wooden shoon, the stomachers and quaint head gear of the familiar pictures have given way to more modern garb. On this island, however, the tourist finds them as they were centuries ago. Of course, it is profitable for these islanders, as things are now, to maintain a style of dress which attracts the tourist and his money. But originally the cause was not commercial. Remote from the mainland and left to their own devices, customs and traditions became ingrained. From generation to generation habits of living were transmitted without change, the decorum to be observed at all village ceremonies became prescribed and a permanent fashion in dress was established.

We may find a parallel to these conditions, although in a milder degree, in our own country. The New England village in winter is an isolated community. Not infrequently the farmhouses themselves are distances apart. Day after day the farmer sees the snow-covered fields and hillocks, does the same round of "chores" in the same way, and contracts his social life to an occasional "party" or "church-fair." He becomes awkward in his ways when out of the beaten path of his

life, uncongenial to strangers and taciturn of manner. In a vista so narrow and limited, prejudices
and antipathies thrive. Neighbors become bitter
enemies over trifles and the feuds last long because
there is plenty of time on the part of both to
brood over each fancied slight and grievance.
Gossip is retailed with zest, because anything is
welcomed that breaks up the deadly, almost soul-
killing monotony. The silent tragedies of spinsterhood and of dreary domestic existence are
played over and over again. This may sound very
gloomy and pessimistic. I do not deny that there
is a brighter side but it exists in spite of the isolation to which the farmer and his family are sub-
jected.

The modifying effects of climate on man are too
well known to need much comment. In the South
Sea Islands the native lazily squats under his co-
coanut tree and waits for the nuts to drop. He is
congenitally shiftless. Owing to the fact that good
labor is so difficult to secure, the mineral resources
of South America remain undeveloped. Liberia,
the negro republic in West Africa, has a climate
which is considered among the hottest in the world.
As a result it has lapsed into a primitive barbar-
ism although its founders were American negroes.
A recent traveler reports that the warship given
by the German government lies rotting in the
principal harbor and that conveying freight on
one's head is still a favorite means of transporta-

tion. The country is in an undeveloped condition because the individual units, the citizens, are entirely too lazy to take hold of the government firmly. This is entirely due to climate.

In the extreme north, industry suffers on account of the intense cold. The Esquimo leaves his oil-heated snow hut only when he must, to obtain food. In the temperate climates, where the rigors of heat and cold are not extreme, we find civilization at its highest efficiency and the greatest initiative among men.

Buckle in his "History of Civilization in England" says: "Climate influences labor not only by enervating the laborer or invigorating him, but also by the effect it produces upon the regularity of his habits."[1] He claims that people of northern climates as well as those of the south lack the habits of steady industry so characteristic of people in temperate climates. In illustration he cites the people of Sweden and Norway on the one hand and those of Portugal and Spain on the other.

In lands where there is constant contact with the terrible aspects of nature, great gales and earthquakes, the imagination of the inhabitants is heightened. Frequently it takes the form of superstitions. The innumerable legends about tutelary saints in Italy, Spain and Portugal illustrate this tendency. Heightened imagination, however,

[1] Buckle: "History of Civilization in England," Vol. I, Chap. II.

here takes another turn in the direction of art. The countries mentioned can boast of many great names in painting and sculpture, among them some of the very greatest: Raffaello, Angelo, Murillo and Velasquez.

As illustrating differences among peoples due to natural causes among them, climate and fertility of the soil, Buckle cites a parallel between India and Greece. In the former, man being constantly eclipsed by nature permitted his imagination to roam wildly. He created as gods monsters of unspeakable terror (Siva). In Greece, on the other hand, where nature proved less formidable, man conceived gods in his own image (Apollo, Jupiter).

The topography of a country adds its influence to that of climate in determining the nature of the inhabitants. People dwelling in mountain regions are almost always liberty loving and independent. The verdure-clad mountains rising to the skies inspire freedom. The constant, successful battle with nature makes the people hardy and self-reliant. Barren, flat stretches such as the deserts of Arizona and Sahara are generally uninhabited although frequently used in transit. Death stalks over the sands and fills with terror the souls of those who must face him as a part of the day's work. The stories of the desert and their own experiences tend to excite superstition and fatalism.

Sterility of soil in countries affects the population noticeably. Where the means of livelihood is so hard to obtain, the settlements are thin and scattered. In consequence educational institutions and the refining influences of society as agents in the development of character are negligible quantities. Men grow up like cactus plants with a minimum of culture. This is true of undeveloped or newly developing communities, as well as those that have become dwarfed, stunted or static on account of the sterility of the soil. But the reverse is also true.

Where the soil is well drained and climatic influences are congenial to agriculture, thriving communities spring up. Our great Middle West owes its wealth to the vast areas devoted to grain growing. The vicinity of large towns renders civilizing and refining influences easy of access. In our own country, where a great foreign element is engaged in the cultivation of the soil, the type of the older generation differs from that of the younger. The gap between the old and the young widens. Problems of adjustment spring up and many tense situations are created. The student of human nature, the writer, seizes upon these aspects for the creation of dramatic stories. Hamlin Garland in his excellent little collection, "Main Travelled Roads" has made a study of this type. In the days when the Mississippi boats plied up and down the river the life on the decks became markedly characteristic. Mark Twain, in his entertaining volume, "Life on the Mississippi" treats this phase.

The kinds of industries adopted by people vary with their proximity to bodies of water. Important cities like Chicago, New Orleans and New York owe their prosperity to the fact of favorable geographic location. They themselves radiate their influence over vast areas in their vicinity. They become art centers, literary centers,—broadly speaking, culture centers. In some cases, as, for instance, in the case of New York, a city assumes a commanding position over the entire country. From the Atlantic to the Pacific, from the Great Lakes to the Mexican border its financial operations and its art products send wave on wave of influence into countless human lives. Where the population is congested into a comparatively narrow area, social problems arise. The difference between the rich and the poor is greatly intensified, because, on the one hand, the opportunities for spending wealth in a city are very numerous and the possibilities of degradation almost unlimited. In the social and moral scale there always seems to be a one step lower. Thus countless types are created, running a human gauntlet from the luxury-wearied and pleasure-bored aristocrat to the flotsam and jetsam of the city streets, the human wrecks that form on the bread line after midnight.

We have dwelt so far on the effects of isolation,

climate and topography on the human character. We have seen how man is reshaped in his manner of living through agencies beyond his control. It remains to be seen how the interplay of man and man and the influence of man-made institutions, industries and occupations affect the individual and collective units of humanity.

In the early days of '49 when canvas-covered wagons followed a long trail westward to the gold mines of California, the far West had not yet found itself. Every incoming caravan brought a new host of adventurers. Law and order were not firmly established. A rough justice prevailed which often proved more cruel than it intended to be. In the new life all possible tendencies for good and for evil had free play. If a man desired to go to the devil he could go his own way provided he did not shoulder the wrong man once too often. The lust for gold and the love of woman, the pride of the pioneer, the rage of the whisky-maddened brute, the justice of the redwood gallows,—all played their part in the new theater of dazzling opportunities, sudden wealth and baffled hopes. No wonder that the vogue of wild-west fiction lasts so long. There are so many romantic and realistic combinations possible that an author of even moderate fertility of invention never finds a dearth of picturesque material in that quarter.[1]

[1] See "The Outcasts of Poker Flat"—Bret Harte.

The cotton fields of the South not only favored a typical community life on the part of the negro but an ingrained aristocratic exclusiveness on the part of their masters. The former, wallowing about in the cabins of the negro quarter, lived a life of animal satisfaction. Sometimes plaintive and sad, their voices rose to the tunes of the banjo, sometimes in a crescendo of hilarity they screamed encouragement to their buck and wing dancers. The masters, accustomed to being served on every occasion, developed a formalism and courtesy found only in the courts of powerful rulers. With their equals always neighborly, social, convivial, they were patronizing or haughty with their inferiors, as the mood seized them.

The factory towns of the past and present have done their share in modifying and creating types. Life is bounded on both sides by a factory whistle. A monotony of routine prevails in which the human being becomes a mechanism for the production of wealth, hardly a man with the full enjoyment of his powers. Passions are either subdued or break out inordinately. Tragedies are plentiful. Wives and mothers deal with the drink problem in the concrete and all strive to drive the gaunt wolf of poverty a few inches further from the door.

In agricultural areas and in tracts devoted to cow and sheep herding, the typical farmer and the grazer are developed. They are simple folk whose joys are few and elementary, whose round of life familiarizes them with certain set duties which have to be performed. When not within reaching distance of a large town or a city they become men of ingrained characteristics, altogether out of their element, unless they are at their work or talking about it. The short-story writer depicts them either on their native soil or facing for the first time the unfamiliar life of the city. Some of our most picturesque characters in fiction are the cow-punchers of the ranches. O. Henry and Edward Stewart White are only two writers who have seen the possibilities in this field.

The world of business, with its vast machinery of finance is responsible for certain distinctive types. Nowhere are so many human devices employed as for the facilitation of trade. The telephone and the telegraph keep up an interminable toiling. Office buildings rise to dizzy heights and are partitioned off into little coops, in each one of which sits a man or men whose sole object is to manipulate what money they have to make more. Every click of the telegraph, every ring of the telephone, every quotation on the tape of the ticker during business hours makes some modification in someone's fortunes. Employed in undertakings varying from world-wide enterprises to little local deals is a tremendous office force of managers, assistants, clerks, typewriters, stenographers, secretaries, bookkeepers and office boys. The excitement of the financial world is reflected in their movements. The earth revolves about the sun and they revolve in individual orbits about their respective businesses.

When we remember that the human nervous system is very plastic and that it records inalterably the effect of all stimuli exerted upon it we can get some notion of the numerous character combinations possible in fiction. A certain situation will be met in a hundred different ways, depending on the point of view of the principal actor and of the community in which he lives. The world-old passions of love, hate, jealousy, anger, ambition, loyalty, justice, self-sacrifice, depend for their full play on the nature of outer stimuli and on the nature of the reacting human being.

All of the forces outlined here, isolation, climate, topography, industries and occupations change the habits or the nature of man by creating distinctive types. Every distinctive type means a new fictional possibility, for although the emotions themselves are old, a new variant is ever possible. Just as there are no two human beings whose features are exactly alike, so there are no two persons who will meet an emotional crisis in exactly the same way. Locate situations in definite environments with fixed ways of looking at things and fixed modes of living and you will have a study of a concrete human being. The *differentia* will be his own temperament. Without the environment, however, he would be a shadow.

Without it an author could never convey an impression of reality. There is no detail too trifling and no detail too vast for the faithful recording of a human life. Just as the best theater managers look to the numerous *minutiæ* of stage setting to make the drama realistic, so the writer of fiction to make his tale plausible must see his characters not as ghosts moving about in a dream haze but as men of flesh and blood pursuing their callings in definite communities.

Canby truly says in his book, "The Short Story in English," "And as the peculiarly geographical development of our civilization and the general shifting of social standards and social orders which marks the end of the nineteenth century, proceeded, more and more fields were opened up for its (the short story's) use. So after all Harte was right; it was the treatment of life, as it was here in America, which began the vogue of the short story." [1]

[1] Canby: "The Short Story in English," p. 297.

CHAPTER II

THE POINT OF CONTACT BETWEEN THE SHORT STORY AND THE LOCALITY

Now that we have considered the forces that determine localities and types of men and women we are prepared to go a step further. What is the point of contact between the locality and the short story as an art form? Is the localization of a story an essential or a non-essential process? What is gained by giving the characters of our fiction a "local habitation and a name"?

The short-story writer if he is an artist desires to create a definite impression. Since the work of Edgar Allan Poe, beginning with the publication of "Berenice" in 1835 this has been an accepted canon of short-story writing. In his review of "Hawthorne's Tales" Poe says in part: "A skillful literary artist has constructed a tale. If wise, he has not fashioned his thoughts to accommodate his incidents; but having conceived with deliberate care, a certain unique or single *effect* to be wrought out, he then invents such incidents—he then combines such events as may best aid him in establishing his preconceived effect." [1]

[1] *Graham's Magazine*, May, 1835.

In one of the latest and best treatises on "Writing the Short Story,"[1] by J. Berg Esenwein, A.M., Lit.D., the editor of *Lippincott's Monthly Magazine*, a man well acquainted with modern practice, the following law is categorically stated: "The short story produces a singleness of effect denied to the novel."

To produce this effect, however, is no easy matter. It requires a peculiar power to focus all elements that will tend to make the story real within a limited compass. Unlike the novelist the short-story writer cannot build a character laboriously by showing to the reader bit by bit the many concerns of his most intimate life. The introduction to the characters of the short story must be brief and vivid. No surplus detail can be added beyond those barely necessary to bring about the desired effect. And yet the impression must be lifelike. The moment we realize that the short story is one dealing with puppets and marionettes pulled by a visible string we leave the sorry exhibition in disgust. To identify the persons of the fictitious drama with the men and women of the workaday world the writer is forced to show their actions in relation to those of other probable persons. Hence the short story must have a setting.

Locality furnishes a great number of pictur-

---

[1] J. Berg Esenwein, "Writing the Short Story"—Hinds & Noble, 1909.

esque settings. Writers do not hesitate at the present day to make a first hand study of the localities they intend to employ in works of fiction. Kirk Munro, a writer of Juveniles, and Jack London, the novelist, are only two of a great body that travel widely to do this. Nowadays no reputable writer, for instance, would think of writing a short story that deals with the West unless he knows his ground. Fred Lockley, the manager of the *Pacific Monthly* in an article for *The Editor* on "Why They Come Back" quotes from an unsuccessful short story and adds his comment:

"In describing the cowboy the writer says: 'He was clothed in thick ominous buckskin, and at his either side hung pistols, their shining barrels protruding out of their cases. The cowboy looked at the teacher with sheer astoundment and remarked: "Well I'm blowed!" as he fingered one of his shining .42's.' In the first place, I don't know how buckskin would go about it to look ominous; in the next place, they don't have thin, shining barrels. They are blue steel and heavy barreled. Also they don't stick out of their cases for two reasons, the first reason being that the case is called the holster, and the next reason being that the holster is made long enough to fit the barrel,. for the barrel would be sure to catch if it protruded out of the holster. Also, a cowboy usually uses a .44 caliber gun, or 'gat' as they are usually termed. How he could finger a '.42' is a mystery, because no one ever heard of a .42 caliber revolver, for the simple reason they are not manufactured in that size.'' [1]

It is evident that neither the reader nor his guardian, the editor, can be led to mistake a paste jewel for a real diamond. If the short-story writer desires to have a picturesque setting he must know his locality thoroughly. Then his story will have the convincing touch, the atmosphere of reality.

As backgrounds, American writers have used numerous localities. Among those that can be cited for the deep interest they lend to their stories are: "The South in Ante-Bellum Days," "The New England Homestead," "The Mining Town of '49." Writers like Page, Wilkins and Bret Harte have skillfully used the setting as part of the story. The action is not only properly set off but it is directly influenced through the conditions hypothesized by the environment. This will be shown in greater detail later.

The short story, as has been shown, demands unity of effect. It has been shown that the locality helps to secure this by making the setting vivid and real. It has also been indicated how a false touch or ignorance can succeed in destroying the necessary illusion.

At first glance it might seem that the work of Edgar Allan Poe himself is a contradiction to what has been set forth. Poe, it may be argued, is a

[1] *The Editor,* November, 1910, p. 197.

Southern writer, but the creations of his fancy belong nowhere. Locality, therefore, is not the all-important influence in shaping a successful short story.

But such reasoning overlooks the fact that in his works there is a substitute for locality. It is atmosphere. The setting of Poe's stories is in no place on this earth but in a spot consistently built up by his wonderful imagination. One need only begin "The Fall of the House of Usher" to realize that the landscape is veiled in a haze of the author's own making. Somber, melancholy, soul-depressing, it harmonizes with the mood of the story. Crime and sin festering in a human conscience are set off by the dreary marshland, the rotting timbers of the mansion and the dull leaden sky. Locate the story in a happy valley of California, flood it with sunshine and you rob it of all its effect, you exorcise the atmosphere of evil that broods over it and lends it unique distinction. In the "Masque of the Red Death" Poe is forced to invent a wonderful palace with a suite of remarkable rooms, each one decorated in a bizarre chromatic scheme. How much the story gains in power through the vivid picturing of the scene those who have read it can testify. Personally I confess to a thrill whenever I read about the final stand of the prince against the Red Death in the Seventh Chamber, with its tripod of light in the corridor streaming through a red window on the black draperies within.

Poe, therefore, although he did not make use of any definite locality, was forced to employ "atmosphere." It is a poor substitute, however, because Poe's most earnest partisans will not claim for him that he succeeded in investing his stories with the impression of reality. The most that can be said of them from the standpoint of locality is that they obey the laws of their own imaginary domain. Within those limitations they are consistent.

Other demands of short story craftsmanship necessitate a thorough knowledge of the locality in which the story is placed because the short story depends, for verisimilitude, mainly on action and characterization. Locality diversifies both. It supplies a peculiar source of motivation. For example, a girl may wish to remain single in her New England home because her many years of spinsterhood have decided her habits irrevocably. She deliberately breaks an engagement for that reason. She finds that such an act of sacrifice is easy for her. Her New England conscience and the attitude of her fellow villagers toward similar problems render this action probable and realistic. Mary E. Wilkins has given us a very good story about this theme in "A New England Nun." [1]   Bret

[1] Wilkins: "A New England Nun and Other Stories."

Harte's story, "The Outcasts of Poker Flat" [1] would have been improbable anywhere except in its own peculiar setting. A newly settled community expels all the bad people of the town during a sudden wave of reform. These characters are all of a type to be found in the days when the little municipalities of the far West were just springing up. The petty thief, the gambler and the woman of the demi-monde are all very characteristic. A snowstorm arises—one typical of the climate—and the story goes on to its pathetic conclusion. Here the environment, the setting, is decidedly part of the web of the story itself. One cannot be detached from the other without rendering it all flat and insipid.

In one of O. Henry's stories [2] a young man is introduced who makes his living by swindling the people with whom he comes in contact. The scene is laid in the neighborhood of Union Square; the story opens with a view of the park benches and their lolling occupants, takes us to a "flashy" hotel on Broadway and amid the noise of the street cars unravels itself before us. Surely the keen fisher for human dupes is a typical New Yorker. In the roar of traffic his operations are hardly noticed. Here again the locality furnishes the motive, affects the character and is the key to

[1] "Outcasts of Poker Flat" from "The Luck of Roaring Camp"—Bret Harte.
[2] "The Assessor of Success" from "The Four Million"—O. Henry.

the solution of the situation. In all the three instances cited, locality has been both the stimulus and
the scene of plot development.

The point of contact between the short story and
the locality, therefore, is threefold: First, the
locality furnishes a picturesque setting and aids
realism; secondly, the locality makes possible unity
of effect and thirdly it diversifies action and characterization by depicting men and their actions as
affected by a peculiar environment.

The influence of locality in creating the modern
short story has been variously recognized by writers
and critics. A few citations from different sources
will perhaps serve to illustrate some other points
of view.

Mr. Ward Clark, speaking of the widespread use
of local color says:

"Now this cult of the god of local color has
its comic aspects but it is really a sign of health,
and the source of one main merit in all our recent
fiction. It may have led to some wild scrambles
for the unoccupied sites but on the other hand it
has taught many a young author to look for his
material at home, and has signalled to him the
truth that honest, accurate observation will dis-
cover the stuff of fiction anywhere. The true cosmopolite, one remembers, is the man who knows
his own parish. There is as much of the universal
human nature in an Indiana town as in Thackeray's London or Balzac's Paris. And, other things

being equal, the Indiana town has—or at least once had—the advantage for us all of being comparatively fresh and novel. Local color for its own sake has no place in a story; but the history of the human creature in a new environment—that will always afford a vision of possibilities." [1]

Prof. Canby, in his book, "The Short Story in English," attributes the use of local color in the short story to the development of the new technique. He says:

"To say when such narratives begin is to court disaster. Not so uncertain is the time when they became most popular with English and American readers, to wit, the latter part of the nineteenth century.

"It is not hard to understand why local color has played such a part in the short story of this period. The technique invented by Poe is thoroughly adapted to catch and record the superficies of life, and particularly idiosyncrasies of habit, and distinctive qualities of scene. Furthermore, since brevity is essential for good description, the much in little of the nineteenth century short story provides the easiest of means for getting observation into readable form. Again the rising popularity of the short story has been paralleled quite exactly by the growth of interest in special peoples and places." [2]

[1] From *The Bookman*, July, 1910. Article on Stewart Edward White by Ward Clark, p. 487.
[2] Canby: "The Short Story in English," p. 319.

Finally W. L. Courtney in his volume of criticism, ''The Feminine Note in Fiction,'' summarizes the need of locality to the modern short story in these words:

''There must always be something pictorial in the short story. Its art is bound to be some variety of impressionism. Think of the conditions. Within thirty, forty or fifty pages you have to convey to the reader a perfectly distinct and self-centered narrative, idea or impression.'' [1]

[1] W. L. Courtney: "The Feminine Note in Fiction," p. 200.

CHAPTER III

For a long time New England practically meant America. It is not surprising, therefore, that it exercised so profound an influence upon an art form that developed much faster here than in the mother country,—the short story. The first notable interpreter of New England in fiction was Nathaniel Hawthorne.

The faults in Hawthorne's stories, as looked at from the modern standpoint, are obvious. A great deal of irrelevant matter is introduced in the form of description and moralizing. The movement is therefore too frequently retarded. But in spite of these patent defects, his stories possess, along with Poe's, the unity of impressionism which is so essential a characteristic of the good short story of to-day.

In some respects the influence of New England on Hawthorne was greater than that on any one of his contemporaries. The passing of the sterner Puritanism had left its deep trace upon him. The same problems of conscience that stirred his ancestors to a more pronounced dogmatism found in

24

him an artistic expression. It must be remembered
that Hawthorne spent fifty years of his life in one
locality. Aside from the time spent in Europe
when he acted as consul, it will be remembered
that he lived in the neighborhood of Salem, Con-
cord and Boston all his life. In their "History of
Literature in America," Professors Wendell and
Greenough make this statement:

"Thus he grew to be of all our writers the least
imitative, the most surely individual. The circumstances of his life combined with the sensitiveness
of his nature to make his individuality indigenous.
Beyond anyone else he expresses the deepest temper
of that New England race which brought him forth,
and which now, at least in the phases we have
known, seems vanishing from the earth."[1]

Hawthorne was a delicate receptive agent of the
spiritual inheritance of New England,—its over-
wrought religious conscience. Some writers notice
the features of landscape about them, others the
peculiarities, the characteristic traits, the attitude
toward life of the people in their localities. Hawthorne seized the very essence of their natures and
wrought it through his artistry into short stories.
To him the locality in which he lived connoted more
than its "visible forms."

This aspect of Hawthorne's work as well as his
actual observation for literary purposes of the

[1] "History of Literature in America"—Wendell and
Greenough. P. 350. Pub. 1904.

locality in which he lived require some illustration.

"The Gentle Boy" shows Hawthorne's attitude toward Puritan New England. It is a powerful study of Puritan persecution against the Quakers. Highly imaginative though it is, it is true to the spirit of the times. The characters are New Englanders of a bygone generation when a stern and active fanaticism had not yet been replaced by moral rigidity only.

Here is a picture of Puritan intolerance from "The Gentle Boy." Pearson, his wife and the Quaker lad, Ilbrahim, are entering at the church door:

"Pearson and Dorothy separated at the door of the meeting house, and Ilbrahim, being within the years of infancy, was retained under the care of the latter. The wrinkled beldams involved themselves in their rusty cloaks as he passed by; even the mild-featured maidens seemed to dread contamination; and many a stern old man arose and turned his repulsive and unheavenly countenance upon the gentle boy, as if the sanctuary were polluted by his presence. He was a sweet infant of the skies that had strayed away from his home, and all the inhabitants of this miserable world closed up their impure hearts against him, drew back their earth-soiled garments from his touch, and said, 'We are holier than thou.'"[1]

[1] "Twice Told Tales"—A. L. Burt. P. 63.

The desire for martyrdom implanted in the breasts of those exposed to bitter persecution is thus depicted:

"Catherine's fanaticism had become wilder by the sundering of all human ties; and wherever a scourge was lifted, there was she to receive the blow, and whenever a dungeon was unbarred, thither she came to cast herself upon the floor."

In the "Gentle Boy" the conflict is between the harsh Puritan nature and the sweeter, although equally firm, Quaker spirit. Hawthorne's grasp of the feelings manifested by both parties in the unequal combat is masterly.

"The Gray Champion" is a study of the Puritan asserting his rights against the tyrannical government of Andros, the representative of James II.

There is no want of evidence that Hawthorne was a good observer, although his descriptions are ever colored or modified by his fancy. The following stories and sketches are almost purely descriptive, landscape studies through a lens artistically focused: "Little Annie's Ramble," "Rill from the Town Pump," "Sights from a Steeple," "The Village Uncle," and "The Toll-Gatherer's Day." The titles themselves are almost a sufficient index of their contents.

A characteristic bit of description from one of them might not be out of place. It illustrates admirably Hawthorne's peculiar mastery of subjective description. It is taken from "Little Annie's Ramble" and pictures a candy shop:

"Here is a shop to which the recollections of my boyhood as well as present partialities give a peculiar magic. How delightful to let the fancy revel on the dainties of a confectioner—those pies with such white and flaky paste, their contents being a mystery, whether rich mince with whole plums intermixed, or piquant apple delicately rose-flavored; those cakes, heart shaped or round, piled in a lofty pyramid; those sweet little circlets sweetly named kisses; those dark, majestic masses fit to be bridal loaves at the wedding of an heiress, mountains in size, their summits deeply snow covered with sugar. . . . Oh, my mouth waters, little Annie, and so doth yours, but we will not be tempted except to an imaginary feast; so let us hasten onward devouring the vision of a plum cake."[1]

Numerous descriptive passages, written in many moods can be adduced to illustrate the impression which his environment made upon him, spiritually and from the standpoint of subjective observation.

It is true that Hawthorne's sense of locality is dimly suggested but this is to be expected from an author whose characteristic atmosphere is one of half lights and shadows. Perhaps his characters are never real flesh and blood, nor are his scenes highly subjective as they are, other than pictures from the Geography of Dreams. But there is no

---

[1] "Twice Told Tales"—Burt & Co.   P. 103.

doubt whatsoever that the heart of his locality
is in them. There is no doubt that in many of his
short stories and novels he chose models for his
characters from among his own countrymen and
was deeply influenced by the history and fortunes
of New England. In the stories and sketches already named, as well as in many others, he drew
from his own experiences and observations. He
watched the pageant passing before him with the
eye of a dreamer but noted details with the skillful
accuracy of a journalist. Desirous of investing
his work with reality, he kept careful note books.
Fortunately the public has had a chance to study
these in the volumes known as "American Note
Books," in which tiny bits of description, musing
and imagination are jotted down. It is clear that
frequently from these bare hints, Hawthorne built
the finished structure. He made the best of the
enforced provincialism which his long residence
in one section entailed upon him. To Longfellow
he once wrote:

"I have another great difficulty in the lack of
materials for I have seen so little of the world that
I have nothing but thin air to concoct my stories of.
. . . Sometimes, through a peep hole, I have caught
a glimpse of the real world, and the two or three
articles in which I have portrayed these glimpses
please me better than the others."

It is interesting to notice the topics Hawthorne
thought worthy of jotting down in his "Note

Books.'' They are a sufficient index of what in his physical environment impressed him most. For purposes of reference I have classified his first ten topics as to subject matter. They are as follows:

1. A walk to the seashore and back.

2. A walk in North Salem. Weather noted— landscape—children playing.

3. A ride to Boston—a stop at an inn in East Boston—comment on the characters found there.

4. A drive to Nahant—comment on physiognomy —the appearance of the sea—''a hint of a story.''

5. A drive to Ipswich—a country tavern—characters sitting there—a graveyard visit—numerous studies for future stories.

6. Comment on the appearance of oaks in an autumnal wood—on a sermon heard—hints for stories.

7. Principally hints for stories and sketches of a highly fanciful nature.

8. A walk down to the shore in Salem—description of the sky and sea.

9. Comment on the appearance of elm trees in September—miscellaneous reflections suggested by his reading.

10. A walk through Dark Lane and home through the village of Danvers—landscape described—meeting house in Danvers described—miscellaneous thoughts and studies for sketches and stories.[1]

It will be noted that the hints for stories are in-

[1] Hawthorne: "The American Note Books."

terspersed among his other observations. We may
be allowed to draw the inference that Hawthorne
took a great deal of the actual material for short
stories and sketches from personal observation.
The inner significance of his outward world, of
course, received the greatest attention. Of his art
he says himself in what is generally considered one
of his best short stories, "Rappaccini's Daughter" [1]
(referring to Aubepine, the mythical author of the
story, a thinly disguised veil for Hawthorne himself): "His fictions are sometimes historical, sometimes of the present day, and sometimes, as far as
can be discovered, have little or no reference either
to time or space. In any case he generally contents himself with a very slight embroidery of outward manners,—the faintest possible counterfeit
of real life,—and endeavors to create an interest
by some less obvious peculiarity of the subject."
We have seen then that Hawthorne reflects his
environment in his own way, that he understands
its inner life, that he has read aright the Puritan
temperament. In the deepest and fullest sense,
therefore, he has reacted on his locality. We shall
see how the same New England has impressed other
writers, but before going on to them it might not
be amiss to quote a paragraph from a modern critic,
Mr. Robert Morss Lovett, concerning the significance of Hawthorne's short story. He confirms the
idea that Hawthorne was influenced by his locality.

[1] Hawthorne: "Rappaccini's Daughter."

"Hawthorne deals with moral problems and eccentricities of conscience which might be said, like Poe's mechanical horrors, to have no necessary or exclusive home and yet his tales are characteristically and unmistakably of New England. They embody in art that which, in the life of that corner of the world, has most fineness of flavor, and delicacy and distinction and charm. They are the chief contribution of the new world to the world's fiction—absolutely native and national. In their localism too, they set the type which the American short story has in the main followed, in the tales of Miss Wilkins, of Mr. Garland, of Bret Harte, to mention three writers among three hundred."[1]

There are two writers of the pre-modern era (the era of imperfect technique) in New England, who require some mention. They are William Austin and Harriet Beecher Stowe. Neither one is preeminently a great or even a good short-story writer but their work requires some mention because it shows the influence of the older New England.

William Austin is chiefly noted for his story "Peter Rugg, the Missing Man." The main character is partly real, partly mythical, but a great deal of interesting matter is to be found concerning the roads and the inns of the early days. The first part was printed in Buckingham's *New England Galaxy,* September 10, 1824 and it was sev-

[1] Robert Morss Lovett: "On Hawthorne's Short Story" —in *Reader,* August, 1905.

eral times reprinted entire, e. g., in the *Boston Book* for 1841. New York in those days was probably not the center of importance to the country that it is to-day. In the course of the story, Rugg says,

" 'Poh, New York is nothing; though I was never there. I am told you might put all New York in our mill pond (Boston's). No, sir, New York, I assure you, is but a sorry affair; no more to be compared with Boston than a wigwam with a palace.' "

Much more important than this story in reflecting the older New England for us is the work of Harriet Beecher Stowe. Her two volumes, "Oldtown Folks," and "Sam Lawson's Oldtown Fireside Stories" are pictures of a bygone society. The time is about 1800 and the types shown are those of a little Massachusetts village in Norfolk county. They include Indians, Hibernians and English, drawn with sympathy and humor. Since Mrs. Stowe was born in 1812 it is not improbable that her sketches are the result of personal observation.

One character, Sam Lawson, a story teller, runs through all the stories.

The following extract from "The Ghost in the Mill," indicates how scarce reading matter was, especially of the lighter kind.

"In those days we had no magazines and daily papers, each reeling off a serial story. Once a week, *The Columbian Sentinel* came from Boston with its slender stock of news and editorial; but all the multiform devices—pictorial, narrative and poetical—which keep the mind of the present generation ablaze with excitement had not then even an existence. There was no theater, no opera; there were in Oldtown no parties or balls, except, perhaps, the annual election or Thanksgiving festival; and when winter came and the sun went down at half past four o'clock and left the long, dark hours of evening to be provided for, the necessity of amusement became urgent."

The loneliness of early New England is thus depicted:

"In those days of early Massachusetts faith and credence was in the very air. Two thirds of New England was then dark and unbroken forests, through whose tangled paths the mysterious winter wind groaned and shrieked and howled with weird noises and unaccountable clamors. Along the iron-bound shore, the stormful Atlantic raved and thundered, and dashed its moaning waters as if to deaden and deafen any voice that might tell of the settled life of the old civilized world, and shut us forever into the wilderness."

"How to Fight the Devil" is another one of Mrs. Stowe's stories in the same volume. It tells of a practical joke that went astray. The tendency to superstitious belief among the simple New England folk of the early nineteenth century forms the theme of the story. The following paragraph shows how these beliefs affected the nomenclature of places in the neighborhood.

"In almost every New England village the personality of Satan has been acknowledged by calling by his name some particular rock or cave, or other natural object whose singularity would seem to suggest a more than mortal occupancy. 'The Devil's Punch Bowl,' 'The Devil's Wash Bowl,' 'The Devil's Kettle,' 'The Devil's Pulpit,' and 'The Devil's Den,' have been designations that marked places or objects of some striking natural peculiarity. Often these are found in the midst of the most beautiful and romantic scenery, and the sinister name seems to have no effect in lessening its attractions." Unlike Hawthorne's, Mrs. Stowe's interest was mainly pictorial.

We shall now pass on to a group of three writers who have treated of New England in the modern short story. We shall see how each one of these, Miss Wilkins,[1] Miss Jewett and Miss Brown, was impressed by her environment.

[1] Now Mrs. Charles Freeman.

CHAPTER IV

IN MODERN NEW ENGLAND

For some peculiar psychologic reason, the field of New England portraiture has been monopolized by three women. They are Mary Wilkins Freeman, Sarah Orne Jewett and Alice Brown. Perhaps it is because the life of New England with its barrenness of esthetic inspiration has been especially irksome to the more volatile sex. Having made upon them a deeper spiritual impression, it may have found a more ready and more skillful literary expression. But this is merely speculative and suggested by the fact that aside from Hawthorne the New England short story of to-day represents a triumph of feminine achievement.

Since the era of the Puritan, the importance of the purely religious element in the life of New England has dwindled. The bitter fanaticism which condemned men to the stake for differences in creed is gone. The whip, once used liberally on the backs of men, is now employed sparingly even on horses. But character undergoes a slower change than practice. We cannot assume that a few generations have completely transformed, the

Puritan attitude. We must not believe that the tremendous strength of character, which originally drove them to a new country, disappeared after the religious issues, upon which it had been freely exercised, were gone. Take, as an example, a general who has come back from the wars. Although he moves about in a friendly and peaceable social circle, he is still the general. His bearing, his manner, the intonation of his speech are not suddenly dropped. So the strength of the Puritan, his keen religious conscience, once struggling so indomitably with great problems of church and state, is called upon to master the vexing but petty tangles of his domestic and industrial environment.

The New England farmer is a descendant of the Puritan. We must study him to see how the old temperament has changed. To Mrs. Freeman we are indebted for a faithful portrayal of the type. She depicts unsparingly the New England mannerisms and ingrained peculiarities of conscience, will and mind, showing them as a blend of heredity and the conditions of modern life.

It is not my object so much to make an exhaustive study of one author as to find his habitual point of view. It will therefore be more profitable to present intensively a few characteristic stories of Miss Wilkins than to attempt a comprehensive general survey.

"A New England Nun" is the story of a typical old maid, prim and methodical, who had become so used to her single life and its regular routine that the prospect of a change appalls her. She gladly relinquishes an opportunity to marry, because it would take her out of the orbit of habit. With great skill Miss Wilkins pictures her queer little neat ways and her horror of having anything disarranged. The rough boots of a man would work havoc with the carpet and the freshly scoured floor.

The following is a deft bit of characterization:

"She had been peacefully sewing at her sitting-room window all the afternoon. Now she quilted her needle carefully into her work, which she folded precisely, and laid in a basket with her thimble and thread and scissors. Louisa Ellis could not remember that ever in her life she had mislaid one of these little feminine appurtenances, which had become, from long use and constant association, a very part of her personality.

"Louisa tied a green apron round her waist, and got out a flat straw hat with a green ribbon. Then she went into the garden with a little blue crockery bowl to pick some currants for her tea. After the currants were picked she sat on the back door-step and stemmed them, collecting the stems carefully in her apron, and afterwards throwing them into the hencoop. She looked sharply at the grass beside the step to see if any had fallen there."

This is almost a perfect picture of spinsterhood, contented and thoroughly inured to the life of petty duties and observations. We see in such a picture the universal in the particular. Mrs. Freeman has succeeded not in drawing an old maid of her own locality but in sounding the very depth of a spinster's unconscious tragedy. Affection and mother love have been turned into a passion for neatness in trivialities. Where young men of the marrying kind are few and maidens many, such a type is by no means rare.

In another story, "A Gatherer of Simples," this "life force," to use Shaw's expression, takes another turn. Instead of spending itself in a round of domestic duties it turns to an absorbing avocation. The principal character, Aurelia Flower, is a study of a woman with a rich capacity for love almost atrophied under the desiccating influence of a very narrow village environment. She loves her herbs before chance brings human love into her life in the form of a little girl, Myrtie, whom she adopts. In the struggle for the ultimate possession of the child all her pent-up affection bursts out. Lack of wide interests and cheerful society and the stunting effect of a life of routine are well portrayed.

In picturing the delight with which Viny, one of the minor characters, an invalid, hears a bit of news, Mrs. Freeman writes:

"Viny drank in the story as if it had been so much nourishing jelly. Her too narrow life was killing her as much as anything else."

That well-known type, the kitchen drudge, is

the main character in the title story of her volume, "A Humble Romance."

In the introductory paragraphs the girl is shown at her work. The physical results of her protracted toil are vividly portrayed:

"Her finger joints and wrist bones were knotty and out of proportion, her elbows, which her rolled-up sleeves displayed, were pointed and knobby, her shoulders bent, her feet spread beyond their natural bounds—from head to foot she was a little discordant note. She had a pale, peaked face, her scanty, fair hair was strained tightly back and twisted into a tiny knot, and her expression was at once passive and eager."

In its minuteness of detail and intense reality is it not comparable to the justly celebrated paintings of the Dutch masters? Poor Sally appears in all her gauntness, all her pitiful awkwardness. Not an angle nor a straight line nor a hideous knot is softened by the glow of the "light that never was on land or sea." Dull, drab daylight and gray reality!

Her life, however, is sweetened by a touch of romance when she marries a tin peddler.

"Their way still lay through a thinly settled country. The tin peddler found readier customers in those farmers' wives who were far from stores. It was late spring. Often they rode for a mile or two through the lovely fresh woods without coming to a single house.

"The girl had never heard of Arcadia, but all unexpressed to herself she was riding through it under gold-green boughs to the sweet broken jangling of tinware."

The romance is certainly humble, the characters come from a low walk of life but the power of the writer and her sincere grasp of the truth are a constant source of gripping interest.

The story depends for its main interest on the evolution of the soul of a kitchen drudge from the numbness caused by the narrowness and hostility of her farmhouse environment. The stooping figure at the kitchen sink might well be placed side by side with that other delineation of Toil Brutalizing Man—The Man with the Hoe.

One of her very best stories, considered by many to be among the best ever written, is "The Revolt of Mother." As its name indicates it is a study of strained domestic relations. It presents a faithful picture of New England life, narrating the revolt of a woman who had for forty years subjugated her own will to that of her husband. "Father" and "Mother" as well as "Sammy," the son, are reproduced with great fidelity to life. Adoniram, the father, is a man whose way of living had tightened up his tongue and cramped his soul.

He is content to leave his family in sordid quarters while he continues putting up outhouses and sheds for his cattle. He speaks seldom and then but very little. His silence, however, is not the silence of restraint but the silence of a spirit that has been dulled and brutalized by the unvarying sequences of rigorous farm labors.

The opening of the story is impressive. The two main characters at once reveal their natures not only in what they do but in what they fail to do:

" 'Father!'

" 'What is it?'

" 'What are them men diggin' over there in the field for?'

"There was a sudden dropping and enlarging of the old man's face as if some heavy weight had settled therein; he shut his mouth tight and went on harnessing the great bay mare. He hustled the collar on to her neck with a jerk.

" 'Father!'

"The old man slapped the saddle upon the mare's back.

" 'Look here, father, I want to know what them men are diggin' over in the field for, an' I'm goin' to know.'

" 'I wish you'd go into the house, mother, and tend to your own affairs,' the old man said then. He ran his words together and his speech was almost as inarticulate as a growl."

This passage illustrates a type of mind dwelling in a twilight or darkness of its own making. Somber, curt and brutal, Adoniram reflects the deadening of the spirit which results from the daily grind.

From the stories cited, it can be readily seen how Mrs. Freeman's mind reacted on its environment. For downright realism of portrayal and sympathy of touch she is unrivaled in her own group. Her pictures of rural life are almost painful in their fidelity. In a great number of her stories the happiness and suffering of woman is her theme, but she is by no means less able to delineate men, as we have just seen. The Puritan rigidity, soul starvation, and repression of modern New England have been carefully noted by her and artistically limned. Altogether her work is a distinct contribution to the fiction of locality and to American literature.

Miss Sarah Orne Jewett, like Mrs. Freeman, has had her inspiration from New England and recorded her observation in story form with deep sympathy and insight. Her characters, in the main, are in a higher social order than Mrs. Freeman's; her outlook on life is more even, more calm; there is less violence of tragedy and more of happiness in her stories—but, like her, Miss Jewett is an artist of a high order. Seldom does she stray from her Maine villages and New England backgrounds. Her works were recently collected and brought out in a uniform edition. Commenting upon her life-work the reviewer of *The Times* said: [1]

"The people of her books are familiar to us all.

[1] Book Review, "New York Times," Nov. 19, 1910.

Her stories are constructed from material of the most elemental kind: of the pathos incident to old age and loneliness, of the joy of friendship, the peace of quiet paths, of the struggle of trying to make both ends meet, of the humorous development of character where isolation lays its emphasis on heart and mind, or perhaps the odd cranks and whimsies induced by the like cause."

Her story [1] "A Winter Courtship" will give some idea of the characters she chooses for her tales and her attitude toward them.

The stage driver, who is a widower has, as his solitary passenger on a winter journey of seven miles, a woman who is a widow. Mrs. Tobin cleverly manipulates the situation to elicit a proposal from Jefferson. A gentle humor pervades the sketch. The stage driver, who for eighteen years had been traveling the seven miles between Sanscrit Pond and North Kilby, is a vivid bit of characterization. He is depicted as a mild little man who reads blood and thunder stories and carries an unloaded heavy revolver under his front seat cushion. Both he and the scheming old widow, Mrs. Tobin, are typical of their New England surroundings. The sameness in his life is well suggested and also her sense of triumph in getting the man she wanted against the competition of two elderly rivals.

The rigors of a New England winter, as seen

[1] Sarah Orne Jewett: "A Winter Courtship" from "Strangers and Wayfarers."

by Miss Jewett, can be gathered from this paragraph:

" 'Be we got four more (miles) to make? Oh, my laws!' mourned Mrs. Tobin. 'Urge the beast, can't ye, Jeff'son? I ain't used to bein' out in such bleak weather. Seems if I couldn't get my breath. I'm all pinched up and wigglin' with shivers now. 'Tain't no use lettin' the hoss go step-a-ty-step, this fashion.' "

A contrast to this bit of realism and also to the work of Mrs. Freeman is a delicate little sketch called "A White Heron." It is a country idyl of early summer. A little town-bred girl is taken to her grandmother's house in the country and learns to love the birds and little animals that are plentiful near her wild home. While driving the cow home one evening, she meets with a young man who is an ornithologist and has spent the day hunting for birds. He especially seeks information about a white heron. Sylvia thinks she knows the spot where the nest is found, because once she had seen the bird standing in the lush grass of the swamp near the woods. At dawn the next morning she climbs the tallest pine tree in the woods and learns, to a certainty, where the nest is located. The stranger had promised her ten dollars if she could help him find it. In spite of this inducement she decides to maintain silence rather than be the cause of the white heron's death.

The woods at nightfall are thus described:

"The woods were already filled with shadows one June evening, just before eight o'clock, though a bright sunset still glimmered faintly among the trunks of the trees. A little girl was driving home her cow, a plodding, dilatory, provoking creature in her behavior, but a valued companion for all that. They were going away from the western light, and striking deep into the dark woods, but their feet were familiar with the path, and it was no matter whether their eyes could see it or not.''

The beauty and fragrance of the woods affords a fitting setting for this little episode in the life of a wood-child.

Much more grim in its suggestion is a story called "Miss Tempy's Watchers." Two women are acting as watchers at a funeral in a small farming town of New Hampshire. Their characteristic gossip and insight into the lovable character of the deceased furnishes the main interest.

The appearance of the two women is well suggested in this sentence:

"Their faces were interesting—of the dry, shrewd, quick-witted New England type, with thin hair twisted neatly back out of the way."

The sterile nature of most of the farm land is hinted at by Mrs. Crow, one of the women:

" 'Tempy had only ninety dollars a year that came in to her; rest of her livin' she got by helpin' about with what she raised off this little piece o' ground, sand on one side and clay the other.' "

periences were devoid of all human passion, it was
chiefly because they had to be expressed in the
phrase of strict theological usage. There was an
unspoken agreement that feelings of this sort should
be described in a certain way. They were not the
affairs of the hearth and market; they were mat-
ters pertaining to that awful entity called the soul,
and must be dressed in the fine linen which she
herself had elected to wear.''

The description of the village schoolroom in which
the meeting was held is interesting:

''There were the maps of North and South America, the yellowed evergreens, relics of 'Last day,'
still festooned the windows and an intricate 'sum,'
there explained to the uncomprehending admira-
tion of the village fathers, still adorned the black-
board.''

Very similar in theme to Mrs. Freeman's story.
''A New England Nun,'' is Alice Brown's ''A
Second Marriage.'' The former is a study of prim-
ness in an old maid; the latter is a study of the
effects of routine on a married woman. Her husband had just died and her mind had become so
habituated to little tasks, duties and observances
which had become formulated about her late spouse
that she looks with reluctance and later with horror
on a second marriage. In spite of the fact that she
is wooed again by a lover of her youth, she prefers
to remain single for the rest of her life, alone with
her memories. Miss Brown's collection, '' Tiverton

Tales,'' contains specimens of her best work and further illustrations of her point of view.

New England's sterile soil has thus proved fertile to the fiction worker. Although in popularity, stories dealing with the ''Far West'' have always appealed to a wider reading public because of their more obvious spectacular elements, there has always been a quiet following for the domestic story of New England. In Mary E. Wilkins-Freeman. Sarah Orne Jewett and Alice Brown this genre of story has found its ablest exponents and New England her most eloquent interpreters.

CHAPTER V

I.

WE now go further west to see how our common
human nature reacts on a different environment.
The original fund, the good and the bad is always
there. Variations arise because Nature herself presents so many differing phases and because communities of men, in some mysterious way, tend
to create their own standards. Along comes the
unit of life, the individual person, with his native
capacities, meets his environment and is shaped
by it.

Closely akin to Mrs. Freeman's stories of New
England life are those of Hamlin Garland dealing
with the Mississippi valley. The keynote of both
is suffering. Garland presents realistic pictures of
the hard-worked farmer. Overburdened and dull,
plodding day after day through the same round
of arduous and unremunerative toil, he misses most
of the joys that life has to offer. He is a type of
more than twenty years ago, the pioneer Western
farmer. Our deepest sympathies are stirred by the

51

narrative of his soul-stunting drudgery and his heroic though passive endurance.

"Main Travelled Roads" contains six stories, each one powerful. It will be sufficient for our purpose—which is to indicate the author's point of view and the influence of the locality upon his work—merely to subject three of these to careful analysis.

The first story is a "Branch Road," localized in the wheat-growing region of the Mississippi valley. The tragedy has its inception in the jealous rage a lover feels because his sweetheart smiles on others. There follows between the pair a seven-year separation. During that interval she marries a man named Kinney. He is a brute and she becomes a drudge, worn to the bone through the constant housework and the unceasing taunts of her husband and his parents, who live with them. They nag at her continually and make her life almost unendurable through the practice of many insidious meannesses.

The big truth of the narrative lies in the fact that she is typical of a class of unhappy farmers' wives in that locality. Dulled and insensible themselves to anything except the narrow profit and loss and the killing routine of life, the farmers expose those in intimate contact with them to ill treatment and neglect. The woman with her incessant household duties is physically and mentally beaten down. Moral degeneration follows.

The setting is delightfully portrayed. It shows a keen appreciation of nature on the part of the writer, an ability also to seize her happy moods. One feels like using that overworked phrase "the spirit of the West" to describe the sunshine and the exuberance of Nature. But the tragedy is only deepened by contrasting this bounty and happiness with the pitiful, passion-tossed and passion-broken life of man.

It is singularly fitting that when her old lover urges the sickly drudge—his best girl of yore—to run away with him and she at last consents, that the author should reflect the infinity of man's life and its countless phases in a parting touch from Nature.

"She smiled again in spite of herself. Will shuddered with a thrill of fear, she was so weak and worn. But the sun shone on the dazzling, rustling wheat, the fathomless sky, blue as a sea, bent above them—and the world lay before them." [1]

The author's keen observation of his environment is seen in many little descriptive passages. Here is one showing a "wheat thrashing." [2]

"This scene, one of the jolliest and most sociable of the western farm, had a charm quite aside from human companionship. The beautiful yellow straw entering the cylinder; the clear, yellow-brown wheat

[1] From "A Branch Road" in "Main-Travelled Roads," by Hamlin Garland—Stone & Kimball. 1893.
[2] From "A Branch Road" in "Main-Travelled Roads," by Hamlin Garland—Stone & Kimball. 1893.

pulsing out at the side; the broken straw, chaff and dust puffing out in the great stacker; the cheery whistling and calling of the driver; the keen, crisp air, and the bright sun somehow weirdly suggestive of the passage of time.''

"Up the Coulée" is another story of life in the Mississippi valley over which there hangs a Homeric gloom, the gloom of the irretrievable and the fated. Nowhere have I read a short story more directly, almost brutally told, sparing no detail in the wretched life of the small farmer, his pitiful, unceasing, but fruitless battle against his lot. Work, work, work when the sun beats hot and when the rain pours freely out of the swollen clouds. And for what? The mere struggle to exist. The poetry of Nature is lost in the tear-blind sorrow of man.

Two brothers, Howard and Grant McLane meet on the latter's farm in the Mississippi valley. Howard has just returned from the city, a successful actor and dramatist. He is sickened at the misery of the life he had so long left behind him. He makes overtures of friendship to his brother Grant, the one who had remained to work on the farm. The latter is cold and bitter. Then Howard seeks at least to make reparation to his old mother. She readily forgives her son for his long neglect. In an agony of remorse and shame Howard again tries to soften Grant, and at last succeeds. But as they stand together with clasped hands and Grant has refused all offers of help as unavailing, asserting that the opportunities once lost are gone forever, the author leaves us in an atmosphere of predestined misery.

Here is a view of the dullness and sordidness of the farm life.

"As he waited, he could hear a woman's fretful voice, and the impatient jerk and jar of kitchen things indicative of ill temper or worry. The longer he stood absorbing this farm scene with all its sordidness, dullness, triviality and its endless drudgeries, the lower his heart sank. All the joy of the home-coming was gone, when the figure arose from the cow and approached the gate, and put the pail of milk down on the platform by the pump." [1]

Farm work, not of the dainty, pastoral kind that Corydon and Phyllis would delight in, is realistically sketched in the following: [2]

"A farm in the valley! Over the mountains swept jagged, gray, angry, sprawling clouds, sending a freezing thin dizzle of rain as they passed, upon a man following a plow. The horses had a sullen and weary look, and their manes and tails streamed sidewise in the blast. The plow man clad in a ragged gray coat with uncouth, muddy boots upon his feet walked with his head inclined towards the sleet, to shield his face from the cold and sting of it. The soil rolled away black and sticky and with a dull sheen upon it. Near by, a

[1] From "Up the Coulée" in "Main-Travelled Roads."
[2] From the same story.

boy with tears on his cheeks was watching cattle; a
dog seated near, his back to the gale.''

Prosperity had made a deep gap between the
brothers. The one who had remained on the farm
barely eked out his existence; the latter was able to
gratify his whim for every luxury. Garland draws
a final contrast between them as they stood together
in the attitude of reconciliation:

''The two men stood there, face to face, hands
clasped, the one fair-skinned, full-lipped, handsome
in his neat suit; the other tragic, somber in his softened mood, his large, long, rugged Scotch face
bronzed with sun and scarred with wrinkles that had
histories like saber cuts on a veteran, the record of
his battles.'' [1]

Although ''Among the Corn Rows,'' another of
the stories in the same volume, is a comedy, there is
the same recognition of man's struggle for mere
existence against nature and our economic system.
The scene is laid in Dakota and throughout the tale
we are brought in touch with rough men, boisterous,
big hearted and coarse. The tragic strand is again
monotony. It forms a black, straight-ruled pattern
even against the golden background of love.

Imagine a family working in a field under the
following conditions:

''A corn field in July is a hot place. The soil is
hot and dry; the wind comes across the lazily mur-
muring leaves laden with a warm, sickening smell

[1] From ''Up the Coulée'' in ''Main-Travelled Roads.''

drawn from the rapidly growing, broad-flung banners of the corn; the sun nearly vertical, drops a flood of dazzling light and heat upon the field over which the cool shadows run, only to make the heat seem more intense." [1]

In summarizing the work of Mr. Garland for the Mississippi valley, it must be confessed that his power lies in a species of vivid realism.   There is no attempt to gloss over conditions.   It is not in our province in this investigation to probe into economic problems, but the work of Hamlin Garland certainly takes a step in that direction.   Not only has the locality had an influence upon this author.   It has seared its drear hopelessness into his brain.   His are no dainty storiettes dealing with the boredom and finesse of those whose fathers earned fortunes for them; they are the record of homespun lives, the annals of men whose hands are crusty with weather and toil, whose hearts beat on though numb with pain.

William Dean Howells, in the preface to the volume under consideration, has so excellent an appreciation of Garland's work that I may be forgiven for quoting it in part:

"That (Main-Travelled Roads) is what they call the highways in the part of the West that Mr. Garland comes from and writes about; and these stories are full of the bitter and burning dust, the

[1] From "Among the Corn Rows" in "Main-Travelled Roads."

foul and trampled slush of the common avenues of
life, the life of the men who hopelessly and cheer-
lessly make the wealth that enriches the alien and
the idler and impoverishes the producer.

". . . These stories are full of those gaunt,
grim, sordid, pathetic, ferocious figures whom our
satirists find so easy to caricature as Hayseeds, and
whose blind groping for fairer conditions is so
grotesque to the newspapers and so menacing to
politicians. They feel that something is wrong
and they know that the wrong is not theirs; the
type caught in Mr. Garland's book is not pretty;
it is ugly and often ridiculous; but it is heart
breaking in its rude despair." [1]

II.

Edward Stewart White was brought up in the
lumber regions of Michigan and in a great number
of his short stories and novels has dealt with that
locality. "Blazed-Trail Stories" is a collection
treating mainly the life of the lumber worker. Of
the six stories, two are concerned with other phases
of forest life. The titles of the other four, however, indicate the close relation they bear to the lumber industry. They are: "The Riverman," "The
Foreman," "The Scaler," and "The River Boss."
The characters and personalities of the men that
go to make up a lumber camp are well depicted.

[1] Preface to "Main-Travelled Roads." Edition Stone &
Kimball. 1893.

The first story introduces us to "Roaring Dick" Darrel and Jimmy Powers, foreman and riverman respectively. They are both figures of a powerful kind. In the former great skill and agility in big work had been developed, along with an utter unscrupulousness. In the latter a quiet force, equal skill and iron determination. Both are undemonstrative, almost apathetic, but each is capable of rising, if need be, to the sterner virtues. In a "log-birling" contest Darrel fouls Powers and wins. Powers, in his quiet way, promises to get even. During an unforeseen jam in the logs a little later, Darrel's life is in danger. Powers saves him and then dryly explains to his questioner that he had merely saved him for the contest of next year.

The author shows a thorough knowledge of the lumber region and the life of the lumber workers.

Here is a characteristic description of a scene when logs, jammed together, suddenly break apart and begin to float with the current.

"About three o'clock that afternoon, Jimmie's prediction was fulfilled. Without the slightest warning the jam 'pulled.' Usually certain premonitory *cracks*, certain sinkings down, groanings forward, grumblings, shruggings, and sullen, reluctant shiftings of the logs give opportunity for the men to assure their safety. This jam, after inexplicably hanging fire for a week as inexplicably started like a sprinter almost into its full gait. The first few tiers toppled smash into the current, raising a waterspout like that made by a dynamite explosion; the mass behind plunged forward blindly rising and falling, as the integral logs were upended, turned over, thrust one side or forced bodily into the air by the mighty power playing jack straws with them." [1]

The theme of "The Foreman" which follows "The Riverman" is the faithfulness of the Foreman to the firm that hires him. A man named Silver Jack, a saloon owner, had once whipped Richard Darrel while the latter was out on a drinking spree in Bay City. On the strength of this victory, he attempts later to pass liquor to the men of Camp Thirty, in charge of Richard Darrel, while they are at their work. His object is to demoralize the camp, encourage desertions, and reap the profits which the spending of their earnings in his saloon would give him. "That a taste or so of whisky will shiver the patience of men oppressed by long monotony is as A—B—C to the north-country saloon keeper." [2]

In an uneven combat against two men, spurred on by his duty to his firm, Richard Darrel prevails against Silver Jack and his companion and then—

"Richard Darrel painfully cleared his eyes and dragged himself to a sitting position, sweeping the blood of his shallow wound from his forehead. He

[1] From "The Riverman" in "Blazed-Trail Stories," p. 6.
[2] From "The Foreman" in "Blazed-Trail Stories."

searched out the axe. With it he first smashed in the whisky jugs. Then he wrecked the cutter, chopping it savagely until it was reduced to splinters and twisted iron. By the time this was done, his antagonists were in the throes of returning consciousness. He stood over them, dominant, menacing.

" 'You hit th' back trail,' said he, 'damn quick! Don't you let me see you round these diggings again.' . . . And he stood there, huge, menacing against the light—the dominant spirit, Roaring Dick of the woods, the incarnation of necessity, the Man defending his Work, the Foreman." [1]

The Foreman's duties toward the firm are here valued as more important than life itself. "Roaring Dick" Darrel, going on a prolonged drunk himself during the off season is one person; Richard Darrel smashing the whisky jugs because they would cripple the efficiency of the workers at his camp, another. The Work becomes the Man.

The next study is that of the "Scaler," a man whose work plays an important part in the management of a lumber camp. We shall permit the author to recount the scaler's duties for us:

"His business was by measuring the diameter of each log, to ascertain and tabulate the number of board feet put in by the contractor. On the basis of his simple report James Bourke, a Foreman, would be paid for the season's work. Inevitably

[1] From "The Foreman."

he at once became James Bourke's natural enemy, and so of every man in the crew with the possible exception of the cook." [1]

Fitz Patrick, the scaler, insists in the interest of the firm that the logs be cut carefully. Bourke and the men resent the fact that he had "culled" a log which he claimed was useless because it had been improperly cut. They decide to maul him severely. An opportunity arises for them to carry out their designs. Owing to the loose discipline, the men, including the Boss, are all drunk when they beat Fitz Patrick. They leave him frightfully bruised in the snow. The cook finds and resuscitates him. While the former is engaged in making tea, they both notice a wreath of smoke coming from the direction of the men's cabin. In their drunkenness the crew had overturned the stove and set the cottage on fire. The first impulse of Fitz Patrick is revengeful. He will let them burn. The brutes deserve no better fate. He even threatens the cook with physical injury, should the latter dare to help them. Finally he decides to save them, but not from humanitarian motives:

" 'They can go to hell for all of me,' he answered finally, 'but my people want these logs put in this winter, and there's nobody else to put them in.' "

Again faithfulness to the firm and to the work in hand is a dominant theme.

[1] From "The Scaler" in "Blazed-Trail Stories."

In the last of the series, dealing with "The River Boss," the same idea is emphasized. "Jimmy" commits a serious misdemeanor in the eyes of the law in order to get his logs to a certain spot within an appointed time limit.

Edward Stewart White has grasped in these stories the ruling considerations of his locality. He knew the territory well because he had lived in it. He was the first to give expression in fiction to this very picturesque phase of our American life. In each of his stories, it will be noticed, the vocation is revealed as rising dominant over the individual characteristics of the man.

CHAPTER VI

No section of America has received more en-
thusiastic treatment at the hands of her writers
than the South. Her beauty of scenery, her pleas-
ure-loving, semi-indolent life, her graces, her poetry,
her attitudes have all received sympathetic and
loving portrayal.

The book by which George W. Cable is best
known even to this day is the first of a series of
short stories and novels by him, attempting to
picture a phase of life that has passed away, that
of the Creoles of Louisiana. When "Old Creole
Days" was published in 1879 it opened an entrance
into a hitherto unexplored and unexploited field.
The author had an intimate knowledge of the Creole
character and had felt the magic of the peculiar
dialect spoken musically by these half-French natives. For the benefit of those not familiar with
the term "Creole" it might be said right here
that it is used by Cable to signify a white man
or woman, of French descent and untainted by the
admixture of any negro blood.

"Madame Delphine," the opening story has its

setting in the New Orleans of long ago. The
theme is racial,—presenting in the plot development based upon it the rigors of both law and
public opinion against a marriage between a white
man and a woman of mixed blood. The society
of the day is reconstructed for us. The quaint
streets of New Orleans, the rapture of Southern
scenery, the musical *patois* of the natives are all
faithfully reproduced. The locality here as in Mrs.
Freeman's best stories is not only a setting for the
action but an integral part of the motives inciting
the characters. Madame Delphine, the suffering
quadroone; Pere Jerome, the kindly priest; Jean
Thompson, the village notary; Doctor Varillat;
Capitaine le Maitre are all drawn with a truth
of delineation arising from a knowledge of the
neighborhood and the big passions that grew out
of the race question in the South.

One of the best bits of description in the story is
that which pictures a Southern night:

"It was one of those Southern nights under
whose spell all the sterner energies of the mind
cloak themselves and lie down in bivouac, and the
fancy and the imagination that cannot sleep, slip
their fetters and escape, beckoned away from behind every flowering bush and sweet-smelling tree
and every stretch of lonely, half-lighted walk,
by the genius of poetry. The air stirred softly
now and then, and was still again as if the breezes
lifted their expecting pinions and lowered them

once more, awaiting the rising of the moon in a silence, which fell upon the fields, the roads, the gardens, the walls, and the suburban and half-suburban streets, like a pause in worship. And anon she rose.

"Monsieur Vignevielle's steps were bent toward the more central part of the town . . . when, just within this enclosure and almost overhead, in the dark boughs of a large orange tree, a mocking bird began the first low flute notes of his all-night song." [1]

Can love have any more rapturous setting than this? It reminds one of Maupassant's famous sketch "Le clair de la lune" in which a crabbed old priest realizes for the first time why moon-light was given to the earth. This passage reveals Cable as a man who saw his locality through the eyes of a prose poet.

"Posson Jone" in the same volume is another story dealing with the picturesque New Orleans of about 1820. The hero is a Northerner, a parson, who has been entrusted with church funds and has come to New Orleans on a visit. There he meets a typical scamp, Jules St. Ange, who plays the part of a confidence man. He succeeds in getting the parson drunk but fails to get the money which had been stealthily hidden away by the parson's slave. Even in his fall from grace the parson gives such evidences of nobility, that the vol-

[1] From "Madame Delphine" in "Old Creole Days."

atile and emotional Creole, St. Ange, is influenced to begin his reformation.

In the course of the narrative a bull fight is well described, also a gambling den. This sketch like the preceding one gives ample evidence of inspiration for theme and plot development from the life of New Orleans. The local color in all of Cable's stories is, as it were, the flesh and blood of the narrative itself and not merely a garment.

The heroic self-sacrifice of the Creole when occasion calls it forth is the theme of Cable's "Jean-ah-Poquelin." This is a very dramatic story. The action takes place at a time when New Orleans was outgrowing its old bounds, the marshes were being filled up and new streets laid. Jean-ah-Poquelin (the "ah" in the middle by way of derision) resists the progressive invaders to no avail. The reason, as we learn later, is that he had been secretly harboring on his premises a brother who was a leper. The setting, the customs and manners portrayed, form an integral part of the story.

That Cable's success in throwing vivid views of New Orleans upon the screen was not an accident but the result of conscious artistic striving to paint each thing "as he sees it," is attested by Lafcadio Hearn. He says:

"The sharp originality of Mr. Cable's descriptions should have convinced the reader of 'Old Creole Days,' [1] that the scenes of his stories are by

1 *Century Magazine*, November, 1883.

no means fanciful; and the strict perfection of his Creole architecture is readily recognized by all who have resided in New Orleans. Each one of those charming pictures of places—veritable pastels—was painted after some carefully selected model of French or Franco-Spanish origin,—typifying fashions of building which prevailed in Colonial days.''

Canby in ''The Short Story in English'' places the same high estimate on the local color of Cable's work:

''It is the descriptive element, however, which is most valuable in Cable's works: such local color as arises from the unforgettable characterizations of 'Mme. Delphine,' of 'Jean-ah-Poquelin,' of 'Tite Poulette'; the picture of a semi-tropical life and the atmosphere of a vanishing civilization. Next in value is the tender sentiment proper to, and worthy of, such descriptions. Abstract this and the local color from the stories and what have you left?'' [1]

As a final tribute to Mr. Cable's work in local fiction it might be permitted to quote the following high estimate of his achievements by J. K. Wetherill:

''What Bret Harte has done for the stern angularity of Western life, Mr. Cable has wrought, in infinitely finer and subtler lines for his soft-featured and passionate native land. Those who come after him in delineation of Creole character can

[1] Canby: ''The Short Story in English,'' p. 320.

only be followers in his footsteps, for to him alone belongs the credit of striking this new vein, so rich in promise and fulfillment."[1]

Thomas Nelson Page, although also writing of the South has chosen Virginia as the locality for his settings. There is a strain of regret for the passing of the "good old times" in his stories. We are indebted to Page for an excellent portrayal of plantation life in the Southern states. The negro dialect is used as a vehicle for telling these stories.

We turn our attention first to "Meh Lady: A Story of the War," not so much because the plot is exceptionally Southern but because the characters chosen and their manner of speaking is so thoroughly local.

The motif of the story is the faithfulness of Old Uncle Billy, a negro, to his mistress and her daughter. The splendor and affluence and happiness of the old plantation days is touched upon. Desolation, havoc, and war come on. The old plantation is stripped of all its belongings: horses stolen, fields trampled upon, negroes freed or lured away. War in all its horrors is scorching the land.

Patriotism to the Southern cause is revealed at white heat. No sacrifice is too great for its friends and no parley can be had with its enemies. And when, as in this little tale, love and patriotism clash there is material for a story of strong emotion.

[1] In "Authors at Home." Edited by Jeanette and Joseph Gilder—1888. Cassel & Co. P. 57.

Uncle Billy, like Sam in "Marse Chan," is the typical servitor who has grown gray serving his master and mistress and whose allegiance is proof against poverty and the lures of freedom itself. He dreams of the old days almost as the French émigré dreamed of the splendid reign of Louis XIV. Night has fallen over the scene and the old negro muses in these words:

" 'An' dat night when de preacher was gone wid he wife an' Hannah done dropt off to sleep, I was settin' in de do' wid meh pipe, an' I heah 'em settin' dyah on de front steps, dee voices soun'-in' low like bees, an' de moon sort o' meltin' over de yard, and I sort o' got to studyin' an' hit 'pear like de plantation 'live once mo', an' de ain' no more scufflin', an' de ole times done come back agin, an' I heah meh kerridge—horses stomp-in' in de stalls, an' de place all cleared up agin, an' de fence all roun' de pahsture, an' I smell de wet clover-blossoms right good, an' Marse Phil an' Meh Lady done come back an' runnin' all roun' me, climbin' up on meh knees, callin' me "Unc' Billy," an' pesterin' me to go fishin' while somehow Meh Lady an' de Cun'l, settin dyah on de steps wid de voice hummin' low like water runnin' in de' dark—' " [1]

Does not Page seem to be the minstrel of days gone by calling up reminiscence after reminis-

[1] In "In Ole Virginia"—Charles Scribner's Sons. 1892.

cence of the past? The short story, allowing, even demanding a strong impression is a very good medium for that purpose.

A great many critics consider "Marse Chan" to be Page's best story. It is supposedly told to a traveler by an old negro who had been Marse Chan's (Channing's) body servant. The time of the action begins just before the Civil War and ends at the fall of Richmond. It is very dramatically told in negro dialect.

The setting is an old Virginia plantation in antebellum times, also a battlefield. We get a glimpse of plantation life and of the Southern family feuds, which sometimes began over mere trifles and embittered all the members of both families against one another during their progress.

The story illustrates not only the affection of the negro for his master (same theme as in "Meh Lady") but also the sense of honor in the Southern gentleman and the master's devotion to his slaves. One of the incidents is the rescue of a negro slave, Ham Fisher, by his brave master.

The characters are typically Southern. They are as follows: Marse Chan, a fiery blooded, honorable, devoted, courageous Southern gentleman; Miss Anne, a plantation lily, a typical Southern girl, beautiful, imperious, proud of family; Old Colonel Chamberlain, a Southern democrat, an intense partisan, violent in debate; Sam, an old negro body servant of Marse Chan; faithful Judy, Sam's wife and Anne's maid, Marse Chan's parents, a loyal Southern couple.

Although the main theme is romantic love, the story is realistically treated. The author has been at great pains to give a faithful picture of life in Old Virginia even down to the matter of dialect. In a preliminary note, Mr. Page draws a distinction between the negro dialect of Virginia and that of Louisiana. The title of the volume is in itself the best evidence that the source of inspiration for Mr. Page was his native state, Virginia. This is confirmed by reference to "The Old South," his book of essays. A letter found in the breast pocket of a soldier who had been killed at the battle of Seven Pines furnished the seed plot for the story.

"The Old South," to which reference has just been made, contains an essay called "Social Life Before the War."[1] This is written in a vein of regretful memory. The picture drawn seems almost an idealization and yet it has the artist touch of true conviction. Upon reading it we see how subtly yet powerfully the memory of the old life thrilled Mr. Page.

From the essay we gather that the life was one of refinement and hospitality; that the husband adored his wife who was not only his "guide, philosopher, friend," but the head of all his ma-

[1] "Social Life Before the War:" an essay from "The Old South," by T. Nelson Page—Charles Scribner's Sons. 1892.

terial affairs; that the negro, although he worked hard, was contented, happy and looked after. It was, according to Page, a life rich in the blessings of content and good fellowship. The author concludes:

"It has passed from the earth, but it has left its benignant influence behind it to sweeten and to sustain its children. The ivory palaces have been destroyed, but myrrh, aloes, and cassia still breathe amid the dismantled ruins." [1]

Enough has been adduced to show that Page was inspired to his work by the associations of his native state. If the love for the South be the passionate, intense feeling which is his, it is no wonder that even children shouldered arms to protect her when they thought her rights were denied.

A French critic, Madame Thérèse Blanc claims that Page was the first to present the South favorably before the tribunal of the North. She says:

"Des deux cotés il doit y avoir une part d'exagération, de préjugés tout naturels; mais si Mme. Beecher Stowe a gagné triomphalement un grand procès qui était celui de l'humanite tout entiere, le mérite d'avoir rectifié bien des traits grossis pour les besoins de la cause reste a M. Page." [2]

Another writer whom the South "made" is Joel Chandler Harris. If to the short-story reader

[1] From "The South Before the War" in "The Old South," by Thomas Nelson Page.
[2] "Questions Americains," par Mme. Thérèse Blanc. Essay "L'Amerique d'autrefois." P. 65.

Cable stands for Louisiana, and Page for Virginia,
Harris certainly represents Georgia. His knowledge of the home locality is deep, his sympathy
with the negro genuine and profound. Had he
never written anything other than "Uncle Remus"
his position as an interpreter of his native state
and as a writer of national reputation would be
secure. His life was singularly adapted to fit him
for his work. Erastus Brainerd, who contributes
the sketch of "Joel Chandler Harris" for "Authors
at Home," in speaking of his personal habits says:

"For amusement he hunted rabbits with a pack
of half-bred harriers, or listened to the tales of
the plantation negro, who was there to be found in
primitive perfection of type. It was on the Turner
plantation that the original 'Uncle Remus' told
his stories to the little boy. So it was that he
absorbed the wonderfully complete stores of knowledge of the negro which have since given him fame.
He heard the negro's stories and enjoyed them, observed his characteristics and appreciated them." [1]

He enjoyed the privilege of studying his characters first hand. Through this, he was enabled to
write his masterpiece, "Uncle Remus," which shows
so intimate a knowledge of the negro and his point
of view.

The legends of "Uncle Remus" are the truest expression of the negro character. "Uncle Tom's
Cabin" as a novel and "My Old Kentucky Home"

[1] In "Authors at Home"—Jeannette L. Gilder.

as a song are both idealizations. Neither one is popular with the negro. Both represent the white man's dream for him. But in the stories of "Uncle Remus," Brer Rabbit is his own hero. The mixture of shrewdness and helplessness perhaps gives the ingredients in the character of the plantation negro himself.

Uncle Remus is a slave who is favored by his mistress because he had seen her grow up from childhood to womanhood. The little Boy whose questions elicit his delightful stories is probably a son of the master. In a series of legends Uncle Remus recounts the adventures of Brer Rabbit, Brer Fox, Brer Coon and many other animals. These creatures are but thinly disguised, individualized human beings. It is the negro himself who under the mask of the various animals reveals his own interesting personality.

His traits as we see them through the medium of "Uncle Remus" are as follows: He is superstitious, credulous, a good story teller, a good singer, mildly arrogant on account of self-esteem arising from his position in the household, faithful to his mistress and master, a lover of children and a handy man of all work.

The duties of Uncle Remus were sundry and varied. Being the household favorite he was given general supervision over all things and free rein to do as he pleased. In "How the Birds Talk" his services are enumerated:

"He did no great amount of work, but he was never wholly idle. He tanned leather, he made shoes, he manufactured horse collars, fish baskets, foot mats, scouring mops, and ax handles for sale; he had his own watermelon and cotton patches; he fed the hogs, looked after the cows and sheep, and, in short, was the busiest person on the plantation." [1]

The *dramatis personæ* of these sketches are the possum, coon, polecat, owl, rabbit, wolf, snake, mink, buzzard and terrapin. The setting is sometimes a plantation and sometimes a swamp. Each animal is strongly individual in character. I have attempted to get the essential attribute of each one. Judging them from their actions in all of the stories they may be classified as follows:

1. Brer Rabbit: shrewd, roguish.
2. Brer Fox: thievish, tricky, not generally successful.
3. Brer Wolf: a gourmand, clumsy.
4. Brer Polecat: arrogant.
5. Brer Owl: mysterious.
6. Brer Snake: sleek, revengeful.
7. Brer Buzzard: a knave, but good natured.
8. Brer Terrapin: stupid.

It will be seen at a glance that this array of animals is portrayed from direct observation of various negro types.

[1] "How the Birds Talk," p. 109, in "Daddy Jake, the Runaway."

The value of these sketches as a contribution to American literature has by no means been overlooked. In discussing the standing of Joel Chandler Harris in American literature William Malone Baskervill, a Southern critic says:

". . . to Putnam County was awarded the honor of giving birth to 'Uncle Remus,' a veritable Ethiopian Æsop, philosopher and gentleman, and to the 'Little Boy' whose inexhaustible curiosity and eagerness to hear a 'story' have called forth the most valuable and in the writer's opinion, the most permanent contribution to American literature in the last quarter of this century." [1]

In another story, "Daddy Jake, the Runaway," [2] Harris departs from his familiar legends to tell a story in which the main character is a runaway slave. "Daddy Jake" belongs to the class of negroes who are very well treated by their masters and completely relied upon. An ignorant overseer ill uses Daddy Jake, so that the latter hits him on the head with a farming implement. The overseer is merely stunned, but the negro believes him dead. He knows the terrible punishment meted out to negroes who strike white men and therefore runs away and hides in Hudson's Cane Brake, a secret meeting place for runaways.

The children of Dr. Gaston, to whom "Daddy"

[1] J. C. Harris, by William Malone Baskervill—Barbee & Smith, Nashville, Tenn. P. 3.
[2] "Daddy Jake, the Runaway"—Century Co. 1889.

belonged, are very lonesome without their old friend
and go "down the river" without the knowledge
of their parents, to search for him. How he is
brought back by them and happiness restored con-
stitutes the rest of the story. Besides "Daddy
Jake" whose faithfulness and love of children are
very characteristic qualities, a woman named
"Crazy Sue" is pictured. She is a half-demented
woman who had been cruelly treated by her master
and had run away. She tells the little children
a story about Brer Rabbit and Brer Coon.

The setting is in Putnam county, the state of
Georgia, in ante-bellum times. We get the spirit
of the big plantation and the "niggers" toiling on
the hot cotton fields. The attitude of the whites
toward them is a mixture of brutality and kindness.

"The Colonel's 'Nigger Dog'" [1] is a story which
shows Harris' mastery of his field. The scene
of action is in Georgia. Unlike Cable's stories,
the setting is not especially emphasized, but the
development of the plot takes into account the
relations between master and slave in the days
before the war. The character of the faithful but
proud negro slave overseer, his domination over
the rest of the negroes, their subservience, Southern
politeness and hospitality are all well portrayed
or suggested. The story relates how the master

[1] From "Tales of the Home Folks in Peace and in War,"
by J. C. Harris.

pursued his erring but faithful slave with a beagle
especially trained to catch negroes.   When he finds
him and is about to lash him severely, the old
family servant hands his master a letter written
by his dead mistress, the present master's mother.
In the letter she tells her son to have great patience
with the negro because of his faithful services to
her. Of course the son relents, the negro is forgiven and peace is established.

In the following passage from "The Colonel's
'Nigger Dog'" we learn how dogs were trained
for negro hunting:

"The colonel trained him assiduously. Twice a
day he'd hold Jeff and make one of the little
negroes run down by the spring-house and out
across the cow lot. When the little negro was well
out of sight the Colonel would unleash Jeff and
away the miniature hunt would go across the fields,
the Colonel cheering it on in regulation style." [1]

"A Baby in the Siege," represents a dramatic
situation at the siege of Atlanta; "The Comedy
of War" portrays a scene between the two con-
flicting parties on neutral ground; "A Bold Deserter," pictures the hardships of conscription in
middle Georgia. Although these and others in the
same volume are good stories showing ability to
handle plot and to suggest suitable backgrounds,
they are not the distinct and individual contribu-

[1] From "The Colonel's 'Nigger Dog,'" by Joel Chandler
Harris.

tion of Joel Chandler Harris to American literature which "Uncle Remus" must ever be. He
will always hold his place along with the other
unperishable characters of fiction.

Thus far we have seen the South through the
eyes of the white men. Fortunately the negro race
itself has produced its own interpreter. Paul Laurence Dunbar, poet and writer of short stories has
told with no mean literary skill of the spiritual,
moral, social and domestic life of the Southern
negro. The book in which most of his prose work
is contained is called "In Old Plantation Days." [1]
In a series of sketches about negroes, he gives brief
snatches and episodes of their lives in short-story
form. They are very subtle in their delineation
of negro character.

The negroes as Paul Laurence Dunbar depicts
them are faithful, shrewd, sentimental and much
given to aping their masters. They are very sus-
ceptible to religious emotion and respond very
readily to the revivalist. The humor and fun of
the old plantation life is well brought out.
Strangely enough (judging from the race of the
author) there is no sentimentality in his stories
and very little subjective writing. Stories are
told accurately and faithfully but objectively. Nowhere does the author intrude himself.

The opening story, "Aunt Tempe's Triumph,"

[1] "In Old Plantation Days," by Paul Laurence Dunbar—
Dodd, Mead & Co. 1903.

is a study of the faithful family servant. She is a plantation "mammy" whose imperious privileges and rights (generically) we have learned to know from the work of Harris and Page. In this case she insists on giving away Miss 'Liza in marriage herself, claiming the privilege as due to her, because she brought her up from infancy. The owner, Stuart Mordaunt, a widower, is represented as being very amenable to her guidance. In another story "Aunt Tempe's Revenge" a negress named Lucy is introduced whose hatreds have a primitive African fierceness.

The emotional negro character is seen to best advantage at a revival meeting. Thus from "In the Walls of Jericho" we get an excellent picture of the negro in the stress of a religious frenzy. A preacher named Johnson uses truly theatrical means to gain and hold his congregation. He has them howling, dancing and eating while they march about imaginary walls of Jericho.

Not only do we get an insight into how the negroes spent their spare time from "How Brother Parker Fell from Grace," but we also get an unusually well-defined portrait of a typical negro preacher. In the heat of his zeal for reforming his flock, Brother Parker steals into a smokehouse and catches some of his parishioners playing cards on Sunday. One of the culprits, Mandy's Jim, accuses the preacher of denouncing card playing because he himself had been unsuccessful at it.

Angry at the taunt, the Preacher declares that he can play better than Mandy's Jim and is willing to prove it "fu' de Gospel's sake."

While they are playing at high-low-jack, Brother Parker's master appears and puts the wrong construction on the scene. All is afterwards explained and Brother Parker is exonerated. His zeal and ruffled dignity are well portrayed. Brother Parker, who is willing to play with Satan for the sake of the Lord, is a most delightful creation.

Lastly we get the comedy of plantation life in "The Trouble About Sophiny" and "A Supper by Proxy." The former deals with the question of social primacy between the Butler and the Coachman. Both desire to invite Sophiny, a negro waiting maid to a ball given by the "Quarters." It is decided that the question of who should ask her first be decided fistically. When the battle has been waged, much to their mutual harm, they are chargrined to find that a field hand, Sam, had anticipated both of them and had been accepted by the fickle Sophiny. In "A Supper by Proxy," the negro butler, Anderson, pompously impersonates his master during the latter's supposed absence, but is caught at it, much to his discomfiture.

Paul Laurence Dunbar has faithfully presented the aspects of the life he saw, the life of which he himself was a part. He is the only author who has given us the negro in the short story from the negro's own standpoint. It is surprising to find how very much akin his point of view is to that of the white writers. He sees the lights and the shadows, the humors and the sorrows, the comedies and the tragedies of the negro quarter both fairly and sympathetically. Skillfully, he avoids the pitfall of sentimentality, writing with an artistic restraint and an objectivity which are in every way admirable.

CHAPTER VII

IN KENTUCKY AND TENNESSEE

THE fame of James Lane Allen rests mainly upon his strong Kentucky novels but in his short-story work as well he emphasizes the fact that the locality can furnish considerable stimulus and inspiration to a writer.

"Flute and Violin" is the name of a volume that contains a collection of stories. They all deal with his native country, the blue-grass region of Kentucky, and its picturesque folk.

In the title story, the main character is a Kentucky parson. He is shown in the midst of his parish working quietly, kindly in spirit and solicitous of his parishioners' welfare. His struggles to have the church endowed are typical of any small community. The place of the action is Lexington, Kentucky, and the time, at the end of the eighteenth and the beginning of the nineteenth century. The parson, Reverend Moore, is a simple character who, through an oversight has committed a wrong. The story although true to its locality is only mildly indicative of Allen's strong trend in the direction of Kentucky characterizations and Kentucky word pictures. Far better is another story in the same volume, "King Solomon of Kentucky." The principal character, in mockery called "King Solomon," is a vagrant of Lexington, Kentucky. He is sold in the market place as a shiftless character and bought by a negress, old Aunt Charlotte. She has memories of King Solomon as a neighbor of her former master's. A pestilence breaks out upon the town. Even the gravediggers flee. Seized by a sudden noble resolution, King Solomon, the vagrant, decides to stay, takes his mattock and spade and inters the dead who otherwise would have been left unburied.

The characters of the story, typical of Kentucky, are:

1. King Solomon, originally a Virginian who had migrated to Kentucky and fallen upon evil ways.

2. Aunt Charlotte, an old negress, the personification of faithfulness. This characteristic is especially emphasized by all Southern writers.

3. Adolphe Xaupi, a dancing master.

4. The Sheriff who conducts the slave sale.

5. Medical students, a happy, irresponsible lot who are present at the sale.

The action takes place at the time when Henry Clay was in his prime. The status of the town is indicated in the following sentence from the story:

"Yes, the summer of 1833 was at hand, and there must be new pleasures, new luxuries; for

Lexington was the Athens of the West and the Kentucky Birmingham.''[1]

But the best of all the stories in the volume and one especially indicative of Allen's peculiar strength is ''Two Gentlemen of Kentucky.'' It is a pathetic narrative of the relations existing between a faithful slave and his former master. Old Colonel Fields stands out like a portrait of Rembrandt's: quaint, gentle, polite, his vision turned toward the past. Peter Cotton, the former slave and negro preacher is hardly less distinct. The splendors of the old régime—of the happy, plantation life under the reign of a kind master are sympathetically portrayed. Wheat fields, singing negro laborers, the gentle old colonel and his faithful body servant, blend together in a harmonious picture. Like Page's stories of Virginia it breathes a sigh for the passing of the old times, but with an implied acknowledgment that the new era is rightfully in its place.

The descriptions of the blue-grass country are admirably done, especially the scene when the Colonel leaves his old homestead. There is a poetic fervor in each reminiscent detail:

''The Eternal Power seemed to have quitted the universe and left all Nature folded in the calm of the Eternal Peace. Around the pale-blue dome of the heavens, a few pearl-colored clouds hung

[1] From "King Solomon of Kentucky" in "Flute and Violin," by James Lane Allen.

motionless, as though the wind had been withdrawn to other skies. Not a crimson leaf floated downward through the soft silvery light that filled the atmosphere and created the sense of lonely, unimaginable spaces. The light overhung the far-rolling landscape of field and meadow and wood, crowning with faint radiance the remoter low-swelling hilltops and deepening into dreamy shadows on their eastern slopes.'' [1]

This is a description in which words are veritable artists' pigments. A man who writes like this must have felt the magic of his native scenes. Colonel Fields revolves the old times in his memory. Once more the magic of the old life is thrown over them. He sees the old plantation as it was:

''. . . The silent fields around him seemed again alive with negroes singing as they followed the plows down the corn rows or swung the cradles through the bearded wheat. Again in a frenzy of merriment the strains of the old fiddles issued from crevices of cabin doors to the rhythmic beat of hands and feet that shook the rafters and roof. Now he was sitting on his porch, and one little negro was blackening his shoes, another leading his saddle horse to the stiles, a third bringing his hat, and a fourth handing him a glass of ice-cold sangaree; or now he lay under the locust trees in his yard falling asleep in the drowsy heat of the sum-

[1] From ''Two Gentlemen of Kentucky'' in ''Flute and Violin.''

mer afternoon while one waved over him a bough of pungent walnut leaves, until he lost consciousness, and by and by awoke to find that they both had fallen asleep side by side on the grass and that the abandoned fly-brush lay full across his face."[1]

It is not necessary to quote any further in order to prove the fact that James Lane Allen is a magician of landscape. To him his native fields and hills and valleys are all beautiful and all have a tale to tell. He sees them through a poet's glasses and weaves them into his stories through which they run like threads of purest gold.

This unusual ability to depict the Kentuckian and his land has attracted a great deal of notice from critics. Summarizing his value to the development of the local story in the United States, E. A. Bennett says:

"In reading him one is made conscious of the fact that the United States is not a single country but several. Kentucky, with its glorious grass, its ancient homesteads and hospitality, its Roman delight in fine roads; Kentucky, which, with a population of only two millions, has only one town of over five thousand inhabitants seems as unlike the America of our imagination as old Middle England itself. Indeed, it is a true offshoot of old England, descended by way of Virginia, and one

[1] From "Two Gentlemen of Kentucky" in "Flute and Violin."

has a comfortable suspicion that this, and not roaring New York nor Chicago affronting the skies, is the real, valid America.''[1]

Another tribute to the powers of James Lane Allen is paid by Mr. Mabie:

''Nature furnishes a background of many charming American stories, and finds delicate and effective remembrance in the hands of writers like Miss Jewett and Miss Murfree; but in Mr. Allen's romances, Nature is not behind the action; she is involved in it. Her presence is everywhere; her influence streams through the story; the deep and prodigal beauty which she wears in rural Kentucky shines on every page; the tremendous forces which sweep through her disclose their potency in human passion and impulse.''[2]

From Kentucky to Tennessee is not a very great distance nor is there any discernible gap in the artistry of Charles Egbert Craddock (Miss Mary Noailles Murfree) and James Lane Allen. The former has gathered inspiration from her Tennessee mountains as the latter did from his Kentucky meadows. She has expressed herself through the medium of the short story as he did. Her collection, ''In the Tennessee Mountains'' contains eight studies of the rude mountaineers, reproducing

[1] ''Concerning James Lane Allen'' from ''Fame and Fiction,'' by E. A. Bennett—E. P. Dutton & Co. 1901. P. 174.
[2] Quoted from *The Outlook* by E. F. Harkins in ''Little Pilgrimages.'' Boston: L. C. Page & Co. 1902.

their language and suggesting a tremendous latent power both in the men and in the mountain scenery.

For the actions of men, especially if they lead to somber or tragic consequences, the mountains are an impressive theater. They rear mass upon mass of shaggy sides to the skies. An artist cannot help being impressed by them. But he must have indeed a large brush and a vast imagination to paint their scenes with the necessary heroic stroke. Sunrise and sunset, extending their pageantry of color over crag and chasm, tinting the heights and reaching into the abysses, are the spotlights of God over a stage on which great elemental passions may play their part.

"Drifting Down Lost Creek" is a powerful story in which the mountains and their environment seem more than a setting. Pine Mountain, rising in the distance and never changing, towers cold and inexorable, and the creek winding down from the summit and lost at the base, is like life itself, mysterious, with its happiness vanishing forever to the desolation of mankind. The little odds and ends on the surface, the flotsam and jetsam drifting into that unknown haven are our vanished opportunities or cherished dreams unrealized.

The characters are the inhabitants of the mountains, primitive men and women, leading routine, uneventful lives. Gossip is as dearly relished as in New England, and for the same reason. Civilization has not altogether penetrated; machinery and

agriculture are still crude.   But the mountains are
the home of some natures, steadfast as themselves,
men imbued with great ambitions, women capable
of great self-sacrifice.   The persons in the story are
as follows:

'Vander Price—a young blacksmith, with a talent
for mechanical contrivance.

Cynthia Ware—a simple mountain girl who loves
'Vander Price and makes a great sacrifice for him.

Cynthia's mother—a shrewd mountain woman,
shrewish in temper, smokes a pipe occasionally.

'Vander's parents—very ignorant.   They fail to
understand their son's ambition.   Outlook on the
world is narrow and wrong.[1]

The spoken language of all the characters is the
Tennessee dialect of the whites.   It is more easily
understood by the general reader than the talk
of Page's Virginia negroes.

The opening description is very impressive and
characteristic of the best descriptive touches in
Miss Murfree's work.

"High above Lost Creek Valley towers a wilderness of pine.   So dense is this growth that it masks
the mountain whence it springs.   Even when the
Cumberland spurs to the east are gaunt and bare in
the wintry wind, their deciduous forests denuded,
their crags unveiled and grimly beetling, Pine
mountain remains a somber, changeless mystery; its

[1] From "In the Tennessee Mountains," by Charles Egbert
Craddock (Miss Murfree)—Houghton Mifflin & Co.   1884.

clifty heights are hidden, its chasms and abysses lurk unseen.   Whether the skies are blue or gray, the dark austere line of its summit limits the horizon.   It stands against the west like a barrier."[1]

In theme the story deals with the change that comes over the mountain youth, 'Vander Price, when his mechanical work gains recognition in the town.   It is the old motif: forgotten love and forgotten duties.   The action marches on to its inevitable hopeless conclusion, symbolized by the Creek which winds down the mountain side and mysteriously disappears.

An intensely dramatic gambling story is "Old Sledge at the Settlemint,"[2] with a mountain setting for its action.   There is a good account of a card game played by the mingled light of the moon and the fire of pine knots.   The passion of the loser, his shrieks echoing and reëchoing among the mountains and the weirdness of the entire scene are well described.

Throughout the story are occasional pictures of the mountain scenery that impress the reader with a sense of grandeur and awe-inspiring mystery.

A great social difference sometimes comes between two lives and eventually results in tragic consequences.   If a girl is untutored in all but

[1] From "Drifting Down Lost Creek" in "In the Tennessee Mountains."

[2] From "In the Tennessee Mountains."

mountain lore and her potential lover is a man of culture, the story must take the course that it does in "The Star in the Valley."

To a huntsman camping on a crag at a very high elevation the lighted room of a mountain girl at night appeared as a star in the valley. She is the daughter of a blacksmith, unsophisticated but capable in her own way of rising to great moral heights. She tramps fifteen miles in a snowstorm to save three men from being killed as the result of a deadly feud. Her hopeless, unexpressed love for the hunter—separated from her by abysses of education and social station—is the theme of the story.

Again the authoress shows the inspiration of her mountains. The story is replete with pictures of wild scenery at all seasons. In one paragraph the central idea is clearly defined:

"There are many things that suffer unheeded in those mountains, the birds that freeze on the trees; the wounded deer that leaves its cruel kind to die alone; the despairing flying fox with its pursuing train of savage dogs and men. And the jutting crag whence had shone the camp fire she had so often watched—her star, set forever—looks far over the valley beneath where in one of those sad little rural graveyards she had been laid so long ago." [1]

The other actors in the mountain tragedy be-

[1] From "A Star in the Valley" in "In the Tennessee Mountains."

sides the girl are Jerry Shaw—the drunken black-smith, the girl's father.   Chevis—the sophisticated, dilettante hunter.

In the background one gets a view of the moun-taineers' wives and mothers-in-law, apathetic and silent.

Fifteen years after the appearance of "In the Tennessee Mountains," "The Bushwackers" was published (1899).[1] This is a rather lengthy short story. The setting is in the Tennessee mountains and the action takes place during the war. There are some striking descriptions—especially one of eagles and their brood on a mountain top.

The title is derived from the name given to the band of reckless and irresponsible foragers who plundered both North and South alike. The hero is taken through the greater part of the war and many incidents recounting his bravery are related, including the final episode in which he loses his arm through the rascality of a comrade. That the authoress knows her territory can be readily seen, but that the story is loosely constructed is also —alas—too evident. It seems to lack the unity of her earlier efforts and shows a poor sense of pro-portion. Hilary's love for Delia is a trivial affair as compared with the passion depicted in "Drift-ing Down Lost Creek." All the incidents previous to Hilary's meeting with the Bushwackers and to

[1] "The Bushwhackers," by Miss Mary N. Murfree—Her-bert S. Stone & Co. 1899.

his saving the life of the man who had ruined his arm seem entirely irrelevant in the development of a short story. The expository ending is old-fashioned and inartistic. But in spite of all these faults whatever excellences are to be found are those that come from a thorough knowledge of the locality, its scenes and its characters. Hilary's old mother, who deliberately plans against her son's going to war, is a good bit of characterization.

In "The Panther of Jolton's Ridge,"[1] the subject of illicit distilling is treated. The story deals with the sudden wave of reform that spread over the little mountain community and led to the expulsion of the Brice Brothers, distillers, who frequently became intoxicated with their own products. The plot is well developed through the climax, the firing of the church, in revenge for expulsion from church.

A very good description in the story is that of a train passing at night over a railroad bridge that spans a chasm.

One more story of Miss Murfree's, "Electioneerin' on Big Injun Mounting,"[2] and we must leave the subject. The ignorance of the mountaineer and yet his susceptibility to noble influences is well brought out. Rufe Chadd, a candidate for reëlection as attorney-general has a reputation for extreme severity in the pursuit of justice. He is

---

[1] In "In the Tennessee Mountains."
[2] From "In the Tennessee Mountains."

stabbed by a drunkard, Isaac Bowker, who avows
the deed and is held in captivity. Rufe, in the
expectation of dying, as he gazes at Bowker's worn
wife, tells the spectators that in the event of his
death, Bowker is not to be prosecuted. This turns
the tide of public feeling strongly in his favor.
Rufe Chadd is reëlected by a great.majority.

The following excerpt shows the educational status of the individual mountaineer and of the community:

"There he (Rufe Chadd) had lived seventeen
years in ignorance of the alphabet; he was the
first of his name who could write it. From an
almost primitive state he had overtaken the civilization of Ephesus and Colbury,—no great achievements it might seem to a sophisticated imagination; but the mountains were a hundred years
behind the progress of those centers." [1]

Thanks to Miss Murfree's work in this direction,
the great Smoky Mountains of Tennessee and their
inhabitants have been well delineated. She has
drawn for the bulk of her work from the mountains among which she lived. Of that locality she
is to-day not only the pioneer but also the greatest living interpreter.

---

[1] Page 163—"Electioneerin' on Big Injun Mounting" in
"In the Tennessee Mountains."

CHAPTER VIII

IN THE WEST

SINCE Bret Harte first exploited his unique California before the admiring East, there has never been any dearth of Western stories. The magazines regularly print tales in which the ranch, the cowboy, the bucking bronco and revolver juggling are principal features. Even the moving picture houses—our latest visitation—have featured scenarios dealing with Western life and adventure. It is, of course, impossible to cover the entire scope of what has been accomplished in this field but it is feasible to glance at the work of the famous pioneer, Bret Harte, and some of his better known followers.

First of all, I desire to show that there is a constant call for material dealing with Western themes. It may be assumed that numerous writers exist who are more than ready to gratify this want. The following extracts are taken from a trade manual [1] for writers and specify the needs of the publications mentioned:

[1] "1001 Places to Sell Mss.," p. 62—The Editor Pub. Co., Deposit, N. Y. 1909.

"*Out West*,[1] Los Angeles, Cal.—'Replying to your letter, I would say that the one definite requirement of this magazine is that the matter shall be Western. This requirement is not met by merely locating the story, for example, in the West, but the Westernness must be vital.' "

"*Overland Monthly, The,* San Francisco, Cal.— A magazine of the West; uses stories of pioneer life, adventure, mining. . . .'"

"*Pacific Monthly,* Lafayette B'ld'g, Portland, Ore.—Fiction: Uses love stories if not over sentimental, adventure fiction if of the Western or of the Pacific, storiettes if of Western life, or if not pointedly of any other locality . . . and desires in particular clean and wholesome fiction of Western life and characters."

"*National Magazine,* Boston, Mass.—Fiction: Likes Western, Southern and other settings, but does not care for New England." [2]

Just as the Magna Charta marks an important epoch for the liberties of the English people, so does the appearance of Bret Harte's "The Luck of Roaring Camp" (*Overland Monthly,* 1868) signalize the beginning of the modern American short story that deals with a specific locality. Although short stories of this nature appeared before the publication of "The Luck of Roaring Camp," e. g., "M'Liss" by Bret Harte himself, nevertheless

[1] Page 63, Ibid.
[2] Page 60, Ibid.

their success was merely local. "The Luck" achieved for itself and for its author a national reputation.

Briefly, it is the story of the regeneration of a mining camp through the birth of a little child. It is notable as the first very successful attempt of its author—or of anyone—to transcribe the unusual phases of life and scenery in the gold digging regions into the form of fiction. Its pathos is heightened by the setting of primal woods, gulches, torrents and elemental man, fiercely struggling with his environment. The passions portrayed are naked and gripping, lacking the restraints of civilization but rudely appealing and powerful. The plot development and the final resolution or climax depend for their success upon the wild scenic and human environment in which they take their course. No short story since the day of Hawthorne had made so singularly an American appeal; no short story since the day of Poe showed so much skill and technique. The giant snow-crowned Rockies, the rude cabins of the pioneer settlers, the mêlée of a refugee society give the story not only a realistic background but the unity of impressionism rivaling in class though not in kind, the artistry of "The Fall of the House of Usher."

The description of the various types of men that were to be found in "Roaring Camp" will illustrate Harte's knowledge of his locality and his vividness of characterization:

"The assemblage numbered about a hundred men. One or two of these were actual fugitives from justice, some were criminal, and all were reckless. Physically they exhibited no indication of their past lives and character. The greatest scamp had a Raphael face, with a profusion of blonde hair; Oakhurst, a gambler, had the melancholy air and intellectual abstraction of a Hamlet; the coolest and most courageous man was scarcely over five feet in height, with a soft voice and an embarrassed, timid manner. The term 'roughs' applied to them was a distinction rather than a definition. Perhaps in the minor details of fingers, toes, ears, etc., the camp may have been deficient, but these slight omissions did not detract from their aggregate force. The strongest man had but three fingers on his right hand; the best shot had but one eye."

John Oakhurst, the gambler mentioned in this description, is the chief character in the companion story of "The Outcasts of Poker Flat." All the persons of the story except two are men and women of loose morality. All of them had been exiled from the mining town of Poker Flat, when that town underwent a violent moral regeneration.

The tragedy is heightened by the presence of unsuspected nobility in the dissolute outcasts and the background of mountain scenery looming about them in awe-inspiring grandeur. The crux of the plot is reached through a snowstorm which hedges in the poor victims and subjects them to certain death from starvation.

They look about them, seeking some avenue of escape.

"But it revealed drift on drift of snow piled high around the hut,—a hopeless, uncharted, trackless sea of white lying below the rocky shores to which the castaways still clung."[1]

Thus, with the snow drifting in hopeless masses all about, they perish, innocent and guilty alike, yielding up their lives to nature in one of her cruelest moods.

"Tennessee's Partner" is worthy to take a place beside these two masterpieces of Western delineation. "Tennessee" is the very incarnation of faithfulness. So forcefully is his act of final devotion to a dead comrade (a scoundrel) depicted that we are touched to tears. Almost beast-like, he plods along thinking of nothing but the memory of the man he had befriended—his partner.

One sentence is sufficient to outline the scenic setting:

"And above all this, etched on the dark firmament, rose the Sierra remote and passionless, crowned with remoter passionless stars."[2]

A very interesting publication that gives an excellent idea of what California has meant to its

[1] From "The Luck of Roaring Camp."
[2] From "Tennessee's Partner," by Bret Harte.

writers is called "California Story of the Files."
It was published at the time of the World's Fair
celebration and is in the nature of a trumpet blast
heralding the greatness of that state and its pre-
eminence in letters.   Making all allowances, however, for a little fond exaggeration, it still gives
an excellent idea of California as it impressed its
writers.   It also attempts to define the California
attitude toward them.   The feeling against the
faithfulness of Bret Harte's portrayals is voiced in
this passage:

"But he has remembered things rather strangely,
so Californians think.   He has a wonderful 'Bret
Harte' world of his own that he draws on and
amplifies and turns and twists to suit his literary
purpose.

"If he would only come and sojourn here for
a year, possibly he might get a series of kodaks to
lay away that would give him an entirely new
world to present, much more agreeable, much more
faithful than his old supply, which never were
in quite the right focus." [1]

The editor of the *Argonaut* at that time, Mr.
Jerome A. Hart, gives a lengthy list of short-story
writers who have dealt with various phases of
California life.   The list is interesting inasmuch
as it furnishes some slight indication of the way
writers flock to seize upon the material most familiar to them, to gather inspiration from the scenes

[1] "California Story of the Files"—Pub. 1893.   Mrs. Ella
Sterling Cummins.

of their own homes. To a greater or less extent, a similar list might be compiled for any locality.

Mr. Hart among others, mentions the following writers and the scope of their work:

E. H. Clough: [1] Stories distinctively of the coast —pictures of life in mines, on cattle ranches and in frontier towns.

Mrs. Yda Addis Stork: Another phase of Pacific Coast life, the semi-Spanish civilization.

Sam Davis: Stories of the life of the frontier.

Frank Bailey Millard and Edward Muson: Stories relating to life on the railroad in the railroad towns and with the Indians.

William S. O'Neill: Life on the frontier army posts and among the Indians.

R. L. Ketchum: Stories of the great cattle ranches of Wyoming, Utah and other "Territories" (now states). "His cowboy is the real cowboy and not the fantastic creature of the stage."

E. W. Townsend: Pictures of life in San Francisco.

Turning from California we shall note the work of two representative modern writers who have been influenced by the West, Edward Stewart White and O. Henry. From "Stories of the Wild Life" we can glean some excellent examples of the former's work. (We have already noted his portraits of lumbermen.)

[1] Page 204, Ibid.

"The Girl Who Got Rattled"[1] is a typical Indian story of the West. A young girl in a journey across the plains breaks away from the train of wagons and her absence is noted by one of the guides, Alfred, who spurs to overtake her. Both of them are sighted by Indians. The girl is told to kill herself, should the Indians succeed in murdering her companion. He explains to her how the Indians habitually maltreat their female captives and afterwards expose them to a lingering death. In the fight that follows he stands the Indians off, single handed, through knowing their methods of warfare. An accidental slip of his foot gives the girl, in her excited state, the impression that all is lost. She kills herself in accordance with his warning.

The hero of the story, the guide Alfred, is represented as being a little, bashful fellow, but one in whom true courage was not wanting. The girl, Miss Caldwell, and her fiancé, Allen, are represented as typical Easterners whose idea of "roughing it" is obtained from the comfortable surroundings of the usual camp.

Here is a vivid description of how the Indians rally for fight:

"From various directions, silently, warriors on horseback sprang into sight and moved dignifiedly toward the first corner, forming at the last, a band

[1] "Stories of the Wild Life"—Edward Stewart White. McClure, Phillips & Co. 1904.

of perhaps thirty men. They talked together for
a moment, and then, one by one, at regular inter-
vals, detached themselves and began circling at
full speed to the left throwing themselves behind
their horses and yelling shrill voiced, but firing
no shot as yet.'' [1]

Their method of warfare is outlined as follows:

"Yet there is one thing that can stop them if
skillfully taken advantage of, and that is their lack
of discipline. An Indian will fight hard when
cornered, or when heated by lively resistance, but
he hates to go into it in cold blood. As he nears
the opposing rifle this feeling gets stronger. So
often a man with nerve enough to hold his fire,
can break a fierce charge merely by waiting until
it is within fifty yards or so, and then suddenly
raising the muzzle of his gun. . . . Each savage
knows that but one will fall, but, cold blooded, he
does not want to be that one; and since in such
disciplined fighters it is each for himself, he
promptly ducks behind his mount and circles away
to the right or the left. The whole band swoops
and divides like a flock of swift winged terns on
a windy day.'' [2]

In another story, "Billy's Tenderfoot," Alfred,
the scout, whose bashful, timid manner is mistaken
for lack of grit by people who do not know him,

[1] From "The Girl Who Got Rattled" in "Stories of the
Wild Life," by Edward Stewart White.
[2] Ibid.

gets a commission to take fifty thousand in green-backs from Standing Rock to Spotted Tail. At Billy's tavern there is a hold-up. Alfred would have gotten away safely but Billy's life is threatened by Black Hank, the bandit chief, because he is suspected of having harbored and protected the messenger. At this point Alfred enters, forces all to put down their arms, empties the revolvers in a wonderful display of shooting and rides off with all the horses of the bandits. He promises to leave them and the confiscated firearms at a point along the trail.

This story like others of its class is melodramatic and uses as a source of interest the strange contrasts of a primitive order of society: the sound sleep and the sudden death; the braggart and swaggerer proving a coward; the timid man asserting himself in the moment of trial as a hero. The play of pistols and the hold-ups are added as scenic accessories.

Edward Stewart White's is the Western story as the Easterner likes to read it,—raw, vivid, full of action, excitement and the clicking of guns.

In O. Henry who has also used Western settings for some of his stories we meet a writer who can claim the distinction of being a true cosmopolite. His work reflects his diversified travels. During an eventful lifetime spent in "living" and not in breathing the steam-heated air of a close office, he traveled in many localities and gained inspiration and material from all. He was born at Greensboro, N. C., in 1868, spent two and a half years on a Texas ranch, served as newspaper man, as a sojourner for business reasons in Central America and as a soda water clerk in a drug store. Finally he settled in New York. Here he seems to have drawn his greatest inspiration, as we shall see in the next chapter.

His volume, "Heart of the West," is a collection of stories with a setting in the Western States. A great deal of the material is taken from the life of the Mexican border and the big cattle ranches. The characters are cowpunchers and knockabout agents. The setting furnishes the main plot motives and contributes to the developing incidents. O. Henry's own experience on the Western plain gave him a first hand knowledge of the customs that prevail there. The freedom and ease of the life depicted may be contrasted with the narrower but no less intensely exciting existence of the New Yorker.

"Hearts and Crosses" is a typical story of the West. It tells of the love of a ranch manager who married a cattle king's daughter only to find himself second in command. How the order of precedence was readjusted is the theme of the story. The principal persons are Webb Yeager, the subordinated husband, Baldy Woods, his adviser, a cowpuncher, and Santa Yeager, formerly Santa McAllister, Queen of the Napolito.

The descriptions of horseback riding are especially sympathetic:

"With a pounding rush that sounded like the rise of a covey of quail, the riders sped away toward different points of the compass. A hundred yards on his route, Baldy reined in on the top of a bare knoll, and emitted a yell. He swayed on his horse; had he been on foot the earth would have risen and conquered him; but in the saddle he was a master of equilibrium, and laughed at whisky and despised the center of gravity." [1]

Here is a picture of horseback comrades in Texas:

"At Dry Lake, where their routes diverged, they reined up for a parting cigarette. For miles they had ridden in silence save for the soft drum of the ponies' hoofs on the matted mesquite grass, and the rattle of the chaparral against their wooden stirrups. But in Texas discourse is seldom continuous. You may fill in a mile, a meal, and a murder between your paragraphs without detriment to your thesis. So without apology, Webb offered an addendum to the conversation that had begun ten miles away." [2]

His first hand knowledge of cattle conditions is to be gleaned from this passage. Webb is speaking:

" 'There's a herd of cows and calves,' said he,

[1] From "Hearts and Crosses" in "The Heart of the West," by O. Henry.
[2] Ibid.

'near the Hindo Water-Hole on the Fris that ought to be moved away from timber. Lobos have killed three of the calves. I forgot to leave orders. You'd better tell Simms to attend to it.' "[1]

A night scene on the ranch is briefly but vividly sketched, reminding us somewhat of the famous nocturne in Cable's "Mme. Delphine":

"At midnight Santa slipped softly out of the ranch house, clothed in something dark and plain. She paused for a moment under the live-oak trees. The prairies were somewhat dim, and the moonlight was pale orange, diluted with particles of an impalpable, flying mist. But the mock bird whistled in every bough of vantage; leagues of flowers scented the air and a kindergarten of little shadowy rabbits leaped and played in an open space near by."[2]

What is the Western spirit, we may ask? It is the composite photograph of its men, its animals, its scenery. The tramp and bellowing of cattle—the plains of chaparral, the beat of horses' hoofs on soft mesquite grass, the bellowing of cows as they are branded, the yelping of lobos, the tread of men wearing heavily weaponed belts, the dash and verve of women born to action and power, the picturesque and charming dialect of the half-Mexicans—all these, blended harmoniously and their essence distilled, might stand for the spirit of the West.

---

[1] From "Hearts and Crosses."   [2] Ibid.

In "Telemachus, Friend" occurs a passage worth quoting as showing the means of livelihood adopted by commercial free lances. Hicks, the hotel proprietor, speaks:

" 'I had a friend once of the entitlement of Paisley Fish that I imagined was sealed to me for an endless space of time. Side by side for seven years we had mined, ranched, sold patent churns, herded sheep, took photographs and other things, built wire fences and picked prunes.' " [1]

The humor of O. Henry is the genuine kind that makes you smile both inwardly and outwardly. It is like the dashing of cold water on a forehead hot and pulsing with the day's business, ennui or worries. And the best part of it all is the absolute truth to human nature that dominates all characters no matter in what out-of-the-way or unusual positions they may be thrust. In the "Handbook of Hymen" for instance, the inciting cause is the fact that Sanderson Pratt and Idaho Green are snowbound in the mountains for over three weeks. The resulting disgust of one with the other is humorously depicted. What a contrast, as we shall see, to the brutal realism of Jack London's "In a Far Country" where two men are placed in a similar situation and are thrown solely on each other's companionship.

Sanderson Pratt is telling how they got there:

[1] From "Telemachus, Friend," in "The Heart of the West," by O. Henry.

"We was up in the Bitter Root Mountains over the Montana line prospecting for gold. A chin-whiskered man in Walla-Walla carrying a line of hope as excess baggage, had grubstaked us; and there we was in the foothills pecking away, with enough grub on hand to last an army through a peace conference."

The disgust of the men with each other, a feeling of which Polar explorers have told, is thus indicated in their conversation. Green discourses:

" 'I never exactly heard sour milk dropping out of a balloon on the bottom of a tin pan, but I have an idea it would be music of the spheres compared to this attenuated stream of asphyxiated thought that emanates out of your organs of conversation. The kind of half-masticated noises that you emit every day puts me in mind of a cow's cud, only she's lady enough to keep hers to herself, and you ain't.' "

" 'Mr. Green,' says I, 'you having been a friend of mine once, I have some hesitations in confessing to you that if I had my choice for society between you and a common, yellow, three-legged cur pup, one of the inmates of this here cabin would be wagging a tail just at present.' "

The rest of the story tells how the men find two books and one of them applies the knowledge gleaned from his volume to the winning of a wife.

There have been many writers of Western stories, but most of them have taken as their models, whether consciously or unconsciously the big men such as Harte, White and O. Henry. This does not mean necessarily that the writings of the others are less original but that the work of the three men mentioned is fairly typical of the Western short story be it tragic, serio-comic or altogether humorous. It is becoming increasingly difficult to find a fresh point of view and for that reason the modern writer's product unless it reflects the West as he himself sees it from his own peculiar angle, will prove disappointing and will sound merely as an echo of what someone else has said before.

CHAPTER IX

NEW YORK can hardly be called a single locality since it is made up of so many distinctly individual sections. First we have a well defined division according to wealth. In addition to the more or less prosaic middle class we have the extreme types of the rich and the poor. In addition there are the various nationalities grouped in their own quarters, malodorous, dingy, odd, perhaps, but always picturesque. Thus New York, not being a homogeneous city seems hardly adapted to being artistically circumscribed by one man.

And yet there is a writer who came nearer than anyone else to understanding the New York *motif,* complex as it is. To his observing senses and sympathetic heart its sights, sounds and experiences became blended into a kind of significant composite of wonder. To him the streets were like the thoroughfares of Bagdad through which the good Caliph Haroun al Raschid strolled in search of adventures. Always to him there was something salient, something suggestive, something typical of a great city. He drew freely from its almost inexhaustible stock of characters and portrayed them with a faithfulness that makes them easy to recognize. To O. Henry (Sidney Porter) belongs the distinction of having been the photographer of metropolitan life.

His methods of work were straightforward and effective. He says of himself:

"When I first came to New York I spent a great deal of time knocking around the streets. I did things then I wouldn't think of doing now. I used to walk at all hours of the day and night along the river fronts, through Hell's Kitchen, down the Bowery, dropping into all manner of places, and talking with anyone who would hold converse with me. I have never met anyone but what I could learn something from him; he's had some experiences that I have not had; he sees the world from his own view point. If you go at it in the right way, the chances are that you can extract something of value from him. But whatever else you do, don't flash a pencil and note book; either he will shut up or he will become a Hall Caine." [1]

A story attempting to convey a sense of the surprises New York constantly holds out is "A Little Local Color." [2] The author supposedly goes out with his friend Rivington to see what the Bowery can offer in the way of interesting types. On the sidewalk in front of

[1] *Current Literature*, July, 1910.
[2] "Whirligigs"—Doubleday, Page & Co. 1910.

the club where they had dined, they come upon
two men engaged in an earnest discussion about
political economy. One of these is very "slangy"
in his utterances. The author asks Rivington whether this is not a Bowery tough. He
finds, to his surprise, that the man is a college
professor. They continue to the Bowery where Rivington meets a policeman whom he knows. The
officer points out a young man named Kerry, who,
he says, knows the Bowery very well. Rivington
addresses him in Bowery argot but is astounded
to hear the tough answering him in pure English.
Rivington is very much taken aback but consoles
himself thus:

" 'Well, anyhow, it couldn't have happened anywhere but in little old New York.' "

The flat dwellers, especially the occupants of
cheap furnished rooms are well portrayed in "The
Gift of the Magi."[1]

Jim and Della plan to give each other a Christmas present suitable to the estimate in which a very
loving married couple hold each other. Each one
parts with the thing most dear to get the present,
—she with her precious long hair, he with his only
heirloom, a heavy gold watch. She purchases an
expensive platinum watch chain; he a set of tur-
quoise combs for her lost hair. "Of all who give
and receive gifts," writes O. Henry, "such as they

[1] From "The Four Million"—Doubleday, Page & Co.
April, 1906.

are wisest.   They are the magi.''   The self-sacrifice
of the poor is here the principal theme.

New Yorkers will easily recognize an original
somewhere corresponding to this description from
the same story:

"In the vestibule below was a letter box into
which no letter would go, and an electric button
from which no mortal finger could coax a ring."

That well-known New York institution, the café,
is well drawn.   Note the accurate detail in the following:

"I invoke your consideration of the scene—the
marble-topped tables, the range of leather-uphol-
stered wall seats, the gay company, the ladies
dressed in demi-state toilets, speaking in an ex-
quisite visible chorus of taste, economy, opulence or
art; the sedulous and largess-loving garçons, the
music wisely catering to all with its raids upon
the composers; the melange of talk and laughter—
and, if you will, the Würzburger in the tall glass
cones that bend to your lips as a ripe cherry sways
on its branch to the beak of a robber jay.   I was
told by a sculptor from Mauch Chunk that the
scene was truly Parisian." [1]

In "Between Rounds" O. Henry gives us a view
of a quarrelsome domestic pair in a repertoire of
discord.

The following extract will take us at once into
the midst of the war crash:

[1] From "A Cosmopolite in a Café" in "The Four Million."

" ' "Pigs face" is it?' said Mrs. McCaskey and hurled a stew pan full of bacon and turnips at her lord.

"Mr. McCaskey was no novice at repartee. He knew what should follow the entrée. On the table was a roast sirloin of pork, garnished with sham-rocks. He retorted with this and drew the appropriate return of a bread pudding in an earthen dish. A hunk of Swiss cheese accurately thrown by her husband struck Mrs. McCaskey below one eye. When she replied with a well aimed coffee pot full of a hot, black, semi-fragrant liquid the battle, according to courses, should have ended." [1]

For all the humorous treatment of the quarrel, it is thrown upon the screen sharply and truly. In the same story, New York is characterized half humorously, half seriously:

"Silent, grim, colossal, the big city has ever stood against its revilers. They call it hard as iron; they say that no pulse of pity beats in its bosom; they compare its streets with lonely forests and deserts of lava. But beneath the hard crust of the lobster is found a delectable and luscious food. Perhaps a different simile would have been wiser. Still nobody should take offense. We would call no one a lobster without good and sufficient claws."

There are a great many men and women who, having no ties of kindred in New York City, live in furnished rooms. The desirability of the house,

[1] From "Between Rounds" in "The Four Million."

the room and the treatment depends upon the lodger's purse. In "The Skylight Room"[1] O. Henry pictures for us how the hunter for a "furnished room" is shown around:

"Then—oh, then—if you still stood on one foot, with your hot hand clutching the three moist dollars in your pocket, and hoarsely proclaimed your hideous and culpable poverty, never more would Mrs. Parker be cicerone of yours. She would honk loudly the word 'Clara,' she would show you her back and march downstairs. Then Clara, the colored maid would escort you up the carpeted ladder that served for the fourth flight and show you the Skylight Room. It occupied seven by eight feet of floor space at the middle of the hall. On each side of it was a dark lumber closet or store room.

"In it was an iron cot, a washstand and a chair. Its four bare walls seemed to close in upon you like the sides of a coffin. Your hand crept to your throat; you gasped, you looked up as from a well— and breathed once more. Through the glass of the little skylight you saw a square of blue infinity.

" 'Two dollars, suh,' Clara would say in her half-contemptuous, half-Tuskegeenial tones."

The type that goes to make up New York's great Bohemia of artist would be's, geniuses, pretenders and camp followers is touched upon in "A Service of Love."[2]

1 From "The Four Million."
2 From "A Service of Love" in "The Four Million."

"Joe Larrabee came out of the post-oak flats
of the Middle West pulsing with a genius for pictorial art. At six he drew a picture of the town
pump with a prominent citizen passing it hastily.
This effort was framed and hung in the drug store
window by the side of the ear of corn with an uneven number of rows. At twenty he left for New
York with a flowing necktie and a capital tied up
somewhat closer.

"Delia Caruthers did things in six octaves so
promisingly in a pine tree village in the South,
that her relatives chipped in enough in her chip hat
for her to go 'North' and finish. They could
not see her f—— but that is our story."

The story subsequently relates their struggle to
exist but what interests us most here is the characterization of the pair. We get a glimpse of the
source from which the tawdry Bohemias of lower
New York are being constantly recruited.

Parallel in interest to our Bohemian is the "Man
About Town." Who is he, what does he do, what
does he look like? A newspaper reporter in a
sketch by O. Henry called "Man About Town"
attempts to frame a definition:

" 'Why,' said he, 'a "Man About Town" [1] is
something between a "Rounder" and a "Club-
man." He isn't exactly—well, he fits in between
Mrs. Fish's receptions and private boxing bouts.
He doesn't, well, he doesn't belong either to the

[1] From "A Man About Town" in "The Four Million."

Lotos Club or to the Jerry McGeorghegan Galvanized Iron Workers' Apprentices' Left Hook Chowder Association. I don't exactly know how to describe him to you. You'll see him everywhere there's anything doing. Yes, I suppose he's a type. Dress clothes every evening; knows the ropes; calls every policeman and waiter in town by their first names. No; he never travels with the hydrogen derivatives. You generally see him alone or with another man.' ''

One of the best stories I have read by any author, rivaling the choicest work of de Maupassant in forceful presentation, vividness and suggestiveness is ''An Unfinished Story.''

Here is an impression from it of the streets at night.

''The streets were filled with the rush hour floods of people. The electric lights of Broadway were glowing—calling moths from miles, from leagues, from hundreds of leagues out of darkness around to come in and attend the singeing school. Men in accurate clothes with faces like those carved on cherry stones by the old salts in sailors' homes, turned and stared at Dulcie as she sped unheeding, past them. Manhattan, the night blooming Cereus, was beginning to unfold its dead white, heavy-odored petals.'' [1]

In the streets of this dangerous city walk all types of men. Meanest and vilest of all are the

[1] From ''An Unfinished Story'' in ''The Four Million.''

avowed sensualists and human beasts whose usual prey is the poor shop girl, tired of monotony and crusts, longing for excitement and champagne dinners. A man of this kind is "Piggy" in the same story. The following description is a model of vivid characterization:

"Piggy needs but a word. When the girls named him, an undeserving stigma was cast upon the noble family of swine. The words-of-three-letters-lesson in the old blue spelling book begins with Piggy's biography. He was fat; he had the soul of a rat, the habits of a bat, and the magnanimity of a cat. . . . He wore expensive clothes and was a connoisseur in starvation. He could look at a shop girl and tell you to an hour how long it had been since she had eaten anything more nourishing than marshmallows and tea. He hung about the shopping districts and prowled around in department stores with his invitations to dinner. Men who escort dogs upon the streets at the end of a string look down upon him. He is a type; I can dwell upon him no longer; my pen is not the kind intended for him; I am no carpenter."

Of course this particular story ends unhappily. Piggy's invitation is at last accepted. The author's comment is put in the form of a dream:

"As I said before, I dreamed that I was standing near a crowd of prosperous looking angels, and a policeman took me by the wing and asked if I belonged with them.

" 'Who are they?' I asked.

" 'Why,' said he, 'they are the men who hired working girls and payed 'em five or six dollars a week to live on. Are you one of the bunch?'

" 'Not on your immortality,' said I. 'I'm only the fellow that set fire to an orphan asylum and murdered a blind man for his pennies.' " [1]

It is against the code of the story teller's art to preach a moral lesson. More powerful, however, than an economic exposition of the dangers of starvation wages and more appealing than the most eloquent sermon is this story of Dulcie, the weak, and Piggy, the beast.

A good bit of observation is contained in "Mammon and the Archer." We have all seen a street-blockade such as is described in the following: [2]

"Richard stood in the cab and looked around. He saw a congested flood of wagons, trucks, cabs, vans and street cars filling the vast space where Broadway, Sixth Avenue and Thirty-fourth street cross one another as a twenty-six inch maiden fills her twenty-two inch girdle. And still from all the cross streets they were hurrying and rattling toward the converging point at full speed, and hurling themselves into the struggling mass, locking wheels and adding their drivers' imprecations to the clamor. The entire traffic of Manhattan

[1] From "An Unfinished Story."
[2] From "Mammon and the Archer" in "The Four Million."

seemed to have jammed itself around them. The oldest New Yorker among the thousands of spectators that lined the sidewalks had not witnessed a street blockade of the proportions of this one.''

Let us take a look at Coney Island from O. Henry's fresh view point. The clamorous amusement place is not only perfectly described but the very soul of it is laid bare.

''Brickdust Row''[1] introduces us to a wealthy man named Blinker. He goes to Coney Island where he sees the masses pushing and jostling to enjoy themselves. At first he is repelled, but then the inner meaning of the sight becomes clear to him.

''He no longer saw a mass of Vulgarians seeking gross joys. He now looked clearly upon a hundred thousand true idealists. Their offenses were wiped out. Counterfeit and false though the garish joys of these spangled temples were, he perceived that deep under the gilt surface they offered saving and apposite balm and satisfaction to the restless human heart. Here, at least, was the husk of Romance, the empty but shining casque of chivalry, the breath-catching though safe-guarded dip and flight of adventure, the magic carpet that transports you to the realms of fairyland, though its journey be through but a few poor yards of space. He no longer saw a rabble but his brothers seeking the ideal. There was no magic of poesy here or of art; but the glamour of their imagina-

[1] From "The Trimmed Lamp"—Doubleday, Page & Co.

tion turned yellow calico into cloth of gold and the megaphones into silver trumpets of joy's heralds.''

"The Voice of the City," [1] as its name indicates, attempts to get at the meaning behind the noises of the great metropolis:

". . . To arrive at it we must take the tremendous crash of the chords of the day's traffic, the laughter and music of the night, the solemn tones of Dr. Parkhurst, the ragtime, the weeping, the stealthy hum of cab wheels, the shout of the press agent, the tinkle of fountains on the roof gardens, the hullabaloo of the strawberry vender and the covers of *Everybody's Magazine,* the whispers of the lovers in the parks—all these sounds must go into Voice—not combined, but mixed, and of the mixture an essence made; and of the essence an extract—an audible extract, of which one drop shall form the thing we seek." [2]

Lastly as showing O. Henry's attitude toward the big city whose meaning he read so well, I may cite from the opening paragraph of "The Green Door." [3]

"In the big city the twin spirits, Romance and Adventure, are always abroad seeking worthy wooers. As we roam the streets they slyly peep at us and challenge us in twenty different guises. With-

[1] Title story from "The Voice of the City"—Doubleday, Page & Co. 1909.
[2] From "The Voice of the City."
[3] "The Four Million."

out knowing why, we look up suddenly to see in a window a face that seems to belong to our gallery of intimate portraits; in a sleeping thoroughfare we hear a cry of agony and fear coming from an empty and shattered house; instead of at our familiar curb a cab-driver deposits us before a strange door, which one, with a smile, opens for us and bids us enter; a slip of paper, written upon, flutters down to our feet from the high lattices of Chance; we exchange glances of instantaneous hate, affection and fear with hurrying strangers in the passing crowds; a sudden souse of rain— and our umbrella may be sheltering the daughter of the Full Moon and first cousin of the Sidereal System; at every corner handkerchiefs drop, fingers beckon, eyes besiege, and the lost, the lonely, the rapturous, the mysterious, the perilous changing clues of adventure are slipped into our fingers. But few of us are willing to hold and follow them. We are grown stiff with the ramrod of convention down our backs. We pass on; and some day we come, at the end of a very dull life, to reflect that our romance has been a pallid thing of a marriage or two, a satin rosette kept in a safe deposit drawer, and a lifelong feud with a steam radiator." [1]

There are numerous other stories and sketches that reveal O. Henry's remarkable knowledge of the great metropolis and its human types. I have

[1] From "The Green Door" in "The Four Million."

tried as far as possible in this chapter to reveal him to the reader at first hand, and not secondarily through criticism.

The plots of his stories need not particularly be emphasized. They represent skillful workmanship, it is true, but technique, as such, is outside the province of our discussion. They are almost all cleverly conceived and because the surprise element in them is so prominent, the incidents and situations are frequently bizarre, unusual and very often strained. In a weaker writer this would yield a nonsensical hash; in a writer gifted merely with a pretty fantasy it would entertain but never convince. In the stories of O. Henry, however, the characters are so intensely human, their motives so plausible and above all, the setting is so realistic that we are whirled along in the sweep of the tale, fascinated and convinced. It is a New York, pulsing with life, that he pictures, a New York that can be woefully prosaic or imbued with an atmosphere of the wildest romance. Coney Island, the cheap eating house, the furnished room, the tenement flat, the café illuminated with "one-thousand candle power," the sidewalks of Broadway,—all yield him their stories. Artists, philistines, hoboes, cabbies, shopgirls and men-about-town form a delightful stock company for the enactment of brief comedies and tragedies arising from the problems of their occupation and position in society. The magician's wand has touched them all, for they are their natural selves and disport themselves with a freedom and vivacity usually not seen in private individuals appearing in important rôles before a critical audience.

O. Henry differs from all others who have taken New York as a setting in the respect that he possessed a far broader range of vision than any one of them. He is not content to single out one neighborhood and exhaust all its fictional possibilities. In the great hocus-pocus of the city he saw unity. Types, sounds, sights, adventures all coalesced and from the blend came that remarkable product—the O. Henry story.

It is too early to predict his place in literature. O. Henry is almost too vital for any dusty place on the shelf of classics. But if ever keen observation and a fresh view point, as well as vigorous, if sometimes unorthodox, diction, appeal strongly to posterity, O. Henry will not suffer oblivion.

CHAPTER X

THE sense of wonder and the sense of mystery are forever stirred by great polyglot New York. On all sides one hears baffling sounds in unfamiliar languages. Away from his native Russia, the immigrant Jew (on the lower East Side) reconstructs a replica of his former quarters. The Chinaman worships in his own Joss House and indulges his weird, dramatic and musical tastes in his own playhouse. The Greek seeks his brother in the Ice Cream Parlor or in the Florist Shop. The German has his imitation Rathskellers on Broadway; the Frenchman his table-d'hôte restaurants on side streets; the Italian his spaghetti haunts in the heart of his quarter. All indulge in their native pastimes and ceremonials and yet dimly recognize an allegiance to the government that has turned most of them from subjects into citizens. All have newspapers in their own language, retailing the latest happenings in the lands they had left and instructing them in their duties toward the land of their adoption. But like the spectrum of many colors, New York is, after all, a unit. O. Henry's

gaze saw the white harmony. In this chapter I
shall sketch a few writers who have specialized on
the individual tints.

The delineation of school life on the lower East
Side has been a unique contribution of Myra Kelly
to the fiction of New York. When her first volume, ''Little Citizens,'' was issued the public smiled
broadly at the queer sayings and doings of the little
Jewish lads and lassies so grotesquely portrayed.

The first story, ''A Little Matter of Real Estate'' treats of the humors of school life. It illustrates a tangle in the lives of two school children,
cousins, who quarrel because the fathers are on
bad terms with each other over a real estate deal.
The children, Eva and Sadie Gonorowsky annoy
each other in all sorts of ways and Teacher is
distracted at her inability to stop the quarrel. Finally it settles itself. A great fire breaks out in
Nathan Gonorowsky's store. He gets a big sum
of money as insurance and settles his outstanding
debt to his brother. The two little girls get ''glad
on each other.''

The setting is a school on the lower East Side
devoted to the Americanization of Jewish children.
They are represented as talking a mixture of Yid-
dishized English, which, although very funny, is
hardly true to life. It is interesting, however,
when judged as the impression the locality made
on an outsider. It is not in our province to criti-
cise the individual bias of an author toward any

given locality, but merely to establish the fact of
its influence. No two original artists can see a
scene, a situation or a story in exactly the same
way. This must be taken into account whenever
it appears that the writer's point of view differs
from our own conception of the truth.

To give some notion of the peculiar Myra Kelly
dialect, a concoction for which the children are
only partly responsible, we shall listen to Sadie
telling us the cause of the trouble:

" 'Well. Mine uncle he come out of Russia.
From long he come when I was a little bit of
baby. Und he didn't to have no money for buy
a house. So my papa—he's awful kind—he gives
him thousen dollars so he could to buy. Und say,
Teacher, what you think? he don't pays it back.
It *ain't* polite you takes thousen dollars und don't
pays it back . . .

" 'So my papa he writes a letter on my uncle
how he could to pay that thousen dollars. *Goes*
months. *Comes* no thousen dollars. So my papa
he goes on the lawyer und the lawyer he writes
on my uncle a letter how he should to pay. *Goes*
months. Comes no thousen dollars.' " [1]

As a contrast to the foregoing we have another
story in which the author sees the pathos of her
little school world. It is the story of the gift that

[1] From "Little Citizens," by Myra Kelly—McClure,
Phillips & Co. 1904.

the much loved but very poor Morris Mogilewsky gave to his teacher at Christmas time.

The passage recounting the presents given by the children is very true to life. Their uselessness, their miscellaneous nature and the fever with which they are bestowed are equally great:

"Nathan Horowitz presented a small cup and saucer; Isadore Appelbaum bestowed a large calendar for the year before last; Sadie Gonorowsky brought a basket containing a bottle of perfume, a thimble and a bright silk handkerchief; Sara Schrodsky offered a penwiper and a yellow celluloid collar button and Eva Kidansky gave an elaborate nasal douche, under the pleasing delusion that it was an atomizer." [1]

But the contribution of Morris was one that his mother had kissed when his father had handed it to her. He was sure that it must be a very appropriate "present for ladies." It turned out to be the receipt for a month's rent for a room on the top floor of a Monroe street tenement.

Her depiction of school officials whose heads are inflated with a sense of petty power is brutally humorous. Through a peculiar psychologic process the school official very often develops into a pompous, narrow individual. It may be the constant contact with those who must bow before his will or lose their positions; it may be the influence

[1] From "A Christmas Present for a Lady."

of a thousand petty details to which he must give his official attention. Whatever the cause, his soul frequently shrinks until all the humanity and all the milk of human kindness have been wrung out of it.

This particular type of school official is portrayed by Myra Kelly in the person of an Associate Superintendent of Schools, known affectionately by his teachers as "Gum Shoe Tim," due to his stealth in ferreting out a teacher's shortcomings. On his approval or disapproval, teachers' licenses were renewed or canceled. His methods, in this instance, are especially brutal:

"He had almost finished his examinations at the nearest school where, during a brisk campaign of eight days, he had caused five dismissals, nine cases of nervous exhaustion, and an epidemic of hysteria."

Myra Kelly in the story, "Morris and the Honorable Tim" [1] gives a vivid delineation of this opinionated and power-bloated official.

In the narrow confines of her chosen field she has worked sincerely. But I leave her with the caution that it is a Myra Kelly world we are reading about and not, strictly speaking, the school world of the lower East Side. The self-sacrifice, the nobility, the ambition shining out through the fogs of poverty and despair—she has not touched

[1] From "Morris and the Honorable Tim" in "Little Citizens."

upon. With the gift of a rich sense of humor she
has dwelt upon the foibles of language and of
manner that have differentiated the Jewish type
from all others in this country. Her work is all
too frequently broad burlesque. At times she labors too consciously for contrasts, but, all in all,
her stories show a fair knowledge of conditions
in her school environment and marked ability to
interpret artistically its bizarre picturesqueness.

No American Jew has depicted his people half
as convincingly in their new environment here as
Zangwill has in the old. We have had numerous
short story writers who have dealt with this class
of our citizens. All too many of them were led
astray by the grotesque elements. The conven-
tionalized Jew who cringes, who pronounces his w's
as v's and whose ruling passion is the accumulation
of money is a figure that recurs again and again
in their work.

One of the minor writers who has made an honest
attempt to see the Jew clearly is Bruno Lessing.
He is a Jew himself and came to his task with
an adequate knowledge of the subject and with a
certain degree of natural sympathy. The collection
of stories called ''Children of Men'' is fairly representative of the best he could do.

The opening story of this volume, ''The End
of the Task,'' is, in my opinion, the best. Its

<hr>

1 ''Children of Men''—Bruno Lessing. McClure, Phillips
& Co.

tragic import is driven home through the faithful
description of conditions among the sweatshop
workers.

Braun and Lizschen, lovers, are both toilers in
the same sweatshop. The girl has consumption.
One day he takes her to a free exhibition of paintings "up-town." Their ragged appearance and
foreign timidity incite a museum guard to order
them out. They go, but not before Lizschen's
fancy has been caught by a Corot landscape.
When, shortly after, she becomes very ill, she raves
about this picture. Braun decides to steal it for
her if possible. His attempt is fortunately successful. Lizschen is made happy but does not re-
cover. Upon her death he returns the picture to
the exhibitors but is arrested when he fails to explain how it came into his possession.

Braun is represented as a hard worked pro-
letariat whose finer feelings have been kept alive
by his love for Lizschen in spite of the dulling
monotony and noise of the shop. The girl, Lizschen, is a pale, sickly flower who wilts away in
the close air of the shop.

The constant din of the machinery is thus described:

"The sewing machines whirred like a thousand
devils. You have no idea what a noise thirty sewing machines will make when they are running at
full speed. Each machine is made up of dozens
of little wheels and cogs and levers and ratchets,

and each part tries to pound, scrape, squeak and bang and roar louder than all the others. The old man who went crazy last year in this very same shop used to sit in the cell where they chained him, with his fingers in his ears, to keep out the noise of the sewing machines. He said the incessant din was eating into his brains, and time and again, he tried to dash out those poor brains against a padded wall."[1]

The foregoing paragraph is an example of subjective description that interprets the details it describes. Bruno Lessing saw the tragic phases of the neighborhood clearly.

The Roumanians and the Hungarians, as distinct from the Russian Lithuanians, are "high livers." All over the East Side one may observe their wine cellars and restaurants. In one of his stories, "A Rift in the Cloud" Lessing gives us a good picture of the café devotee.

He is a Hungarian drunkard, Polatschek, and seems to take an odd delight in music. One night while guzzling freely he hears the restaurant orchestra playing the Rakoczy March. A listener comments on how beautifully it was played. Polatschek denies this and seizing the leader's violin plays the march with great dash and fervor.

Here is a glimpse of him in the café interior:

"Night after night he would sit in Natze's Café, where the Gypsies play on Thursdays, drinking

[1] From "The End of the Task."

slivovitz—which is the last stage. He would drink, drink, drink, and never a word to a soul. On music nights he would drink more than usual and his eyes would fill with tears. We all used to think they were maudlin tears, but we had grown accustomed to Polatschek and his strange habits and nobody paid attention to him." [1]

A suggestive little story "Unconverted" takes its theme from the numerous attempts constantly made to convert Jews to Christianity. The Reverend Dr. Gillespie opens a "Mission to the East Side Jews." During his first open air meeting he is struck with a stone on the cheek but is saved from further injury by the intervention of a tall young man. The latter scatters the crowd, stanches the blood upon the Reverend's cheek and invites him up to his rooms on the top floor of an East Side tenement. An old man in the last stages of a wasting illness is lying on a couch.

The young man tells the Reverend the old man's story—a story of self-sacrifice under wrong and true nobility of character. This, he points out, is a real Jew. Those who struck the Reverend Gillespie are renegades to Judaism. He ends up fervently:

" 'Would you convert him? What would you have him believe? To what would you change his faith? Ah, you will say there are not many like

[1] From "A Rift in the Cloud" in "Children of Men."

him. No! would to God there were! It would be a happier world.

" 'But it was faith in Judaism that made him what he was. If I—if all Jews could only believe in the religion of their fathers as he believed— what an 'example to mankind Israel would be!' " [1]

The story ends with this significant paragraph:

"The second outdoor meeting of the 'Reverend Gillespie's mission to the East Side Jews' has never taken place."

Bruno Lessing, because he is a Jew himself, has been able to seize upon and reproduce the unique humor of the Jew. Centuries of persecution have not banished the smile from the Jew's lips. Sometimes he is a conscious, sometimes an unconscious humorist. In both instances he is equally delightful.

"A Swallow-Tailer for Two" is the story of a singular predicament in which Isidore and Moritz were placed because they endeavored to share a dress suit between them during one evening. Moritz promised to give up the suit to Isidore at eleven o'clock for two hours' wear. In the meantime Isidore trails after him to see that the suit should be in perfect condition for him. This is humorously related by Moritz in Yiddish-English dialect:

" 'Efry time I looked around me I seen his

[1] From "Unconverted."

eyes keepin' a lookout on der swallow tail evening dress. Such big eyes Isidore had that night! "Don't vatch me like dot, Izzy," I said. "Dey vill t'ink you are a detectif, unt dot I stole somet'ing." Efry time I drops a leetle tiny bit from a cigar ashes on my swallow tail shirt Izzy comes running up mit a handkerchief und cleans it off. Efry time I sits down on a chair Izzy comes up unt vispers in my ear, "Moritz, please don't get wrinkles in der swallow tail. Remember I got to wear it next. Efry time I took a drink Moritz comes unt holds der handkerchief under der glass so dot der beer should not drop on der swallow tail shirt. "Izzy," I says to him, "I am astonished." ' "

The upshot of it all is that Moritz and Izzy cease to be friends. But the telling of the story rather than the plot is a noteworthy feature. Moritz's humor under stress is especially characteristic of Jewish nature—a shrug of the shoulders and a joke told at one's own expense.

One of the best stories in the volume is "Out of his Orbit." Bruno Lessing in this skit tells of the dire consequences to the individual Jew if he suddenly changes the habits of a lifetime and becomes a drinker.

Mr. Rosenstein, angered by his wife's insistence on obtaining new red wall paper, announces his intention to begin drinking as a means of punishing her. Here is where his troubles begin. Four

Benedictines gulped down at once change this sedate and stationary sphere for Rosenstein. The consequences of his vagary, he finds, are pleasant to all others but frightful to himself. A startling series of mishaps has taken place.

He finds that in the artificial exuberance induced by the spirits, he had dismissed his store staff for a week's holiday, had purchased a white horse to prepare for the opening of a new milk store and among other things had engaged a whole staff of painters to repaper not only the one room his wife desired but the entire suite. His wife is overjoyed and Mr. Rosenstein has not the courage to explain the secret of his generosity. He promises her fervently never to take another drink.

This is the helpless way in which Rosenstein ordered a drink:

" 'Give me a drink,' demanded Rosenstein.

" 'What kind of a drink do you want?' asked the bartender.

"Rosenstein looked bewildered. He did not know one drink from another. He looked at the row of bottles behind the counter, and then his face lit up.

" 'That bottle over there—the big black one.'

"It was Benedictine. The bartender poured some of it into a tiny liqueur glass, but Rosenstein frowned.

" 'I want a drink, I said, not a drop. Fill me a big glass.' "

At this point Rosenstein's life became one of picturesque liveliness and sharp climaxes.

In the stories I have mentioned, Bruno Lessing has caught the double nature of Jewish life, its tragedy on the one hand and its humor on the other. In such tales as "The End of the Task" we feel the utter hopelessness of the sweatshop worker's fate. He is in a worse plight than Hamlin Garland's farmer. The latter at least has the advantage of language. The soil he tills, although it yields him but a bare living, belongs to him. But for the worker on the machine there is no consolation, no respite. He pedals away until the Boss of Bosses summons him. His life is a round of working and sleeping. The din of the machines and the smell of the shop are ever with him.

Besides these serious aspects Bruno Lessing has handled with relish the humors of Jewish life and Jewish character. Sometimes as in the "Americanization of Shadrach Cohen" the fun has an undercurrent of seriousness. The father proves to the children that the command, "Honor thy father and thy mother," applies to the relations between them and him. He outwits them and makes them appear mere tyros in the world of business. In stories like "A Swallow-Tailer for Two," Bruno Lessing's treatment is broad burlesque but nevertheless true to Jewish mannerisms and points of view.

Altogether, although his work falls short of sublimity in treatment and although nowhere, even in his greatest climaxes, does he combine the feeling of reality with a sense of dramatic fitness, nevertheless his stories are drawn from life and are worth reading as a Jew's impressions of Jews.

Brief mention must here be made of a new tendency in fiction. Specialization has gone so far that not only does an author outline a restricted territory for himself on the basis of nationality but even a single occupation within that nationality is made the source of a series of stories. Montague Glass in "Potash and Perlmutter" [1] gives us an entertaining account of the relations between two partners, Abe and Morris, who are cloak and suit manufacturers. All the plots in the book are drawn from that limited field. The book is humorous after a fashion, has some good bits of characterization and touches of commercial philosophy in dialect, but it hardly strikes a high level in the delineation of the Jew. It is mentioned here as reflecting a tendency to further specialization.

Nobody sees New York so comprehensively as the reporter. What he misses in the niceties of style he more than makes up in scope of observation. The training Richard Harding Davis received as a reporter on metropolitan papers had tended to sweep him into many places of interest and had made him feel instinctively what was worth

[1] "Potash and Perlmutter," by Montague Glass—Henry Altemus Co., Pub's.

recording. In the short-story field he has touched upon many phases and has drawn his settings from numerous quarters. There is one field, however, in which he is well-nigh inimitable and that is in the delineation of the New York club-man. His creation, Van Bibber, an apparent dawdler, and yet a man living according to a set code of honor and in the set manner prescribed by his peers in society, is an interesting character. He is not merely a type because Davis was artist enough to give him an individuality of his own but he is sufficiently characteristic to be indicative of the New York club-man's attitude toward life.

"Her First Appearance"[1] is a story in which the darker side of the stage is touched upon. Van Bibber notes a pretty little child making her début in a production of the Lester Comic Opera Co. He knows when he hears her mother's name that the father who had disowned her is a wealthy club-man of his own set. With great difficulty he works upon the father's mind sufficiently to arouse the man's paternal instincts. The father finally acknowledges her.

Van Bibber is impelled to do what he does by the thought that the life of the stage sooner or later contaminates the moral sense. The story is full of references to doings behind the scenes which

[1] "Van Bibber and Others," by R. H. Davis—Harper & Bros. 1892.

make one feel that Davis had gathered material for this story at first hand.

The new production is just being staged and Van Bibber, taking advantage of the license accorded him as an old college chum of Lester's, is wandering about behind the scenes:

"For a moment he hesitated in the crosslights and confusion about him, failing to recognize in their new costumes his old acquaintances of the company; but he saw Kripps, the stage manager, perspiring and in his shirt sleeves as always, wildly waving an arm to someone in the flies, beckoning with the other to the gas man in the front entrance. The stage hands were striking the scene for the first act, and fighting with the set for the second, and dragging out a canvas floor of tessellated marble, and a practical pair of steps over it, and aiming the high quaking walls of a palace and abuse at whoever came in their way."[1]

Carruthers is the obdurate father. He belongs to the type of impassive club-man, who retains his good breeding though violently angry. Even in their lapses from convention it is evident that both he and Van Bibber know the correct form of procedure under the circumstances.

For instance, when Van Bibber tells the reason for his errand to Carruthers, the latter, although

[1] From "Her First Appearance" in "Van Bibber and Others."

deeply hurt, neither scolds nor storms. In a manner chillingly polite he wounds Van Bibber by pointing out to him that his intrusion into another man's affairs is the act either of a cad or a fool. Note the calmness of Carruthers' utterance:

" 'Mr. Van Bibber,' he began, 'you are a very brave young man. You have dared to say to me what those who are my best friends—what even my own family would not dare to say. They are afraid it might hurt me, I suppose. They have some absurd regard for my feelings; they hesitate to touch upon a subject which in no way concerns them, and which they know must be very painful to me. But you have the courage of your convictions; you have no compunctions about tearing open old wounds. . . .' " [1]

The habitual restraint of the well-bred man is here evident even when his anger is at blood heat.

In "Eleanore Cuyler" we get a study of a settlement worker. The big settlements situated in the poor districts of the city draw many of their workers from the ranks of the rich. Eleanore Cuyler is a wealthy young girl who undertakes work in a Rivington Street Settlement after dismissing young Wainwright who intended to propose to her. A thrilling experience is related in which Van Bibber whips three toughs and saves her from insult and perhaps injury. Wainwright, on coming back to New York, gets wind of the story, goes down

[1] From "Her First Appearance."

town, finds his Eleanore in a weary, discouraged mood, due to the numerous difficulties encountered in her work, proposes to her and is accepted.

The "Settlement Worker" type is here well outlined in Eleanore Cuyler. She comes from a wealthy home, has no conception of the problems that are to confront her and seeks to enter the field of settlement work in the spirit of pursuing a philanthropic fad.

Her discouragement just before the coming of Wainwright is thus described:

"She had grown sceptical as to working girls and of the good she did them—or anyone else. It was all terribly dreary and forlorn and she wished she could end it by putting her head on some broad shoulder and by being told that it did not matter, and that she was not to blame if the world would be wicked and its people unrepentant and ungrateful. Corrigan, on the third floor, was drunk again and promised trouble." [1]

The incident of the fight with the toughs is somewhat strained. The strength of the story and of Davis's work in general, lies in his acute reportorial observation. He shows realities to the reader. He reconstructs the environment of a luxurious home as easily as he does an East Side street in the early morning hours:

"From the light of the lamps he could see signs in Hebrew and the double eagle of Russia painted

[1] From "Eleanore Cuyler."

on the windows of the saloons.   Long rows of trucks
and drays stood ranged along the pavements for
the night, and on some of the stoops and fire-
escapes of the tenements a few dwarfish specimens
of the Polish Jew sat squabbling in their native
tongue.'' [1]

A different atmosphere is suggested by the opening paragraph:

''Miss Eleanore Cuyler had dined alone with her
mother that night, and she was now sitting in the
drawing-room near the open fire, with her gloves
and fan on the divan beside her, for she was going
out later to a dance.

''She was reading a somewhat weighty German
review and the contrast which the smartness of
her gown presented to the seriousness of her occupation made her smile slightly as she paused for
a moment to cut the leaves.'' [2]

The valet, as a most necessary adjunct to the
comfortable existence of the club-man, is the theme
of a little story called ''Van Bibber's Man Servant.''

A valet in the employ of Van Bibber is ambitious
to feel the joys of being in his master's place—at
Delmonico's—if only once.   A dinner, ordered by
Van Bibber, suddenly has to be called off.   Walters,
the valet, does not cancel it as he is told to do,
passes himself off as one of the guests, eats the

[1] From ''Eleanore Cuyler.''
[2] Ibid.

dinner and is just enjoying his mint julep and a cigar in the café when Van Bibber comes in.

The spirit of the contented, torpidly self-satisfied life of the restaurants is reflected in this short story—the delight in good dinners, good wines and good cigars which the New Yorker, who dines out, enjoys so much:

". . . It was just the sort of dinner he would have ordered had he ordered it for himself at someone else's expense. He suggested Little Neck clams first, with Chablis, and pea soup and caviare on toast, before the oyster crabs, with Johannisberger Cabinet; then an entrée of calves' brains and rice; then no roast but a bird, cold asparagus with French dressing. Camembert cheese and Turkish coffee. As there were to be no women he omitted the sweets and added three other wines to follow the white wine. It struck him as a particularly well-chosen dinner, and the longer he sat and thought about it the more he wished to test its excellence. And then the people all around him were so bright and happy, and seemed to be enjoying what they had ordered with such a refinement of zest that he felt he would give a great deal could he just sit there as one of them for a brief hour." [1]

In order to write this an author must have felt the spirit of restaurant gayety. It is not enough merely to have read of it in books. The minute

[1] From "Van Bibber's Man Servant."

touches here and there indicate first hand familiarity with the subject—the ordering of the dinner, for instance. Such detail is laboriously gathered as the result of a full life. New York offers countless opportunities to people who want their hours to pass swiftly and gayly.

New York is so vast a subject that there are many other authors who have seen it from still other peculiar angles all their own. Stephen Crane and Owen Kildare were familiar with its dregs; Robert W. Chambers with the decadents of its moneyed class; Edwin Lefevre with its Wall Street gamblers. It is no wonder that there should be so many writers who take New York for a setting. It is an inexhaustible wonderbox of the quaint, the bizarre, the comic, the tragic, the dramatic, the maudlin and the pathetic. Its four million souls work out their destinies in filthy rookeries, in marble palaces, in skyscrapers. Every human passion plays itself out. So that there is an endless variety of subject matter for the writer of the impressionable spirit and the vivid pen.

Thus it happens that the big city has its own fascination for literary folk, as much as the sea or the plain or the forest. For night and day upon its pavements there beats the tread of feet. Night and day within the walls of its buildings, hopes are born afresh and despair claims the weak. So many millions of ganglionic cells plot and toil within it that the eternal quiet which falls daily upon thousands of men never calls a halt to the day's work. The tireless, nervous machine throbs away at its labors like a huge piston on an ocean liner. Truly New York is wonderful and its historians in fiction are like so many Ali Babas knowing a myriad Open-Sesames to a myriad treasure troves of human interest.

CHAPTER XI

A GLIMPSE AT THE FROZEN NORTH: ALASKA

No more fearful setting for human action exists than the bare stretches of ice and snow in the far North. Under its dark sky of a six months' night and its wan sky of a six months' day the most gruesome tragedies can be imagined. It is not a land to thaw out the genial nature in man. It makes him shrink into the warmth of his furs and his snow hut, selfishly glad to be alive. Self-preservation consequently forms a dominating motive and about this theme very many tales dealing with the northland may be grouped.

We may get an adequate idea of the general scope of this type of short story by reading the collection contained in Jack London's volume, "The Son of the Wolf."[1]

The first story, "The White Silence" is a tragedy in which a man known as Malemute Kid is forced to shoot his life-long comrade, Mason, because the latter had been irretrievably injured by a falling pine. The situation is exceedingly tense and dra-

[1] "The Son of the Wolf": Grosset & Dunlap, Publishers—Jack London.

matic because the nearest civilized spot was then
at least two-hundred miles away over a snow trail
that must be traversed with the help of vicious,
starving dogs. Mason's wife, Ruth, is a faithful
Indian woman who meets the tragedy with the
stoicism characteristic of her race.

The agonizing silence of the great snow wastes
broods over the tragedy. Both man and dog have
become elemental brutes and the struggle between
them for mastery is the old one of the beast against
his shrewder captor.

We get a glimpse of the setting from the following:

"The afternoon wore on and with the awe, born
of the White Silence, the voiceless travelers bent to
their work. Nature has many tricks wherewith she
convinces man of his finity,—the ceaseless flow of
the tides, the fury of the storm, the shock of the
earthquake, the long roll of heaven's artillery,—but
the most tremendous, the most stupefying of all,
is the passive phase of the White Silence. All movement ceases, the sky clears, the heavens are as
brass; the slightest whisper seems sacrilege, and man
becomes timid, affrighted at the sound of his own
voice. Sole speck of life journeying across the
ghostly wastes of a dead world, he trembles at his
audacity, realizes that his is a maggot's life, nothing more. Strange thoughts arise, unsummoned,
and the mystery of all things strives for utterance.
And the fear of death, of God, of the universe,

comes over him,—the hope of the resurrection and
the life, the yearning for immortality, the vain
striving of the imprisoned essence—it is then, if
ever, man walks alone with God." [1]

This is certainly an impressive description, written by a man who had evidently experienced the
awesomeness of the White Terror. In the story we
feel all the dread that a sudden death in the Arctic
can inspire.

The title story, "The Son of the Wolf," deals
with the old battle of brain against brawn, of the
barbarian against the European, of civilization
against the primitive. One white man withstands
a hostile tribe of Indians. Scruff Mackenzie desires to win Zarinska, daughter of Thling Tinneh,
Chief of the Sticks. As in the previous story the
theme is the revelation of elemental strength in the
son of the dominant race battling for the possession
of a woman. Shaman, the medicine man of the
Sticks, for reasons of his own antagonistic to Mackenzie instigates a wild dance by women of the
tribe:

"It was a weird scene, an anachronism. To the
South the nineteenth century was reeling off the
few years of its last decade; here flourished man
primeval, a shade removed from the prehistoric
cave dweller, a forgotten fragment of the Elder
World. The tawny wolf-dogs sat between their

[1] From "The White Silence" in "The Son of the Wolf."

skin-clad masters or fought for room, the firelight
cast backward from their red eyes or slavered fangs.
The woods, in ghostly shroud slept on unheeding.
The White Silence, for the moment driven to the
rimming forest, seemed ever crushing inward; the
stars danced with great leaps, as is their wont in
the time of the Great Cold; while the Spirits of
the Pole trailed their robes of glory athwart the
heavens.'' [1]

In a land where man constantly faces the grim
aspects of nature, where death by cold, by starvation and by attacks from hostile tribes is not un-
common, men lose the surface polish of civilized
life and reveal their elemental virtues or their elemental weaknesses. Things are reduced to a fearful simplicity, for the subterfuges of our conventional city life do not obtain in a wilderness of
snow and sky. A man must mean a thing when he
says it. He must do his part of the community
work with sheer faithfulness. Explanations, ex-
cuses, apologies are not wanted. In a state of
society where it is necessary to counteract so de-
termined an opposition on the part of nature to
the comfort of man, the work of the individual,
if left undone, leaves a gap through which the
forces of destruction may enter. The justice of
the wilderness is therefore not a thing of legal
quibbles and oratory. It is dealt out directly in

[1] From "The Son of the Wolf."

primitive fashion. Death is the punishment for most offenses,—death to the man whose life mars the happiness or welfare of his brethren.

Another element that enters into the life of the dweller in the Arctic wastes is Chance. A man will undertake an enterprise if there is a fighting chance for its success. He will face grave danger if there is a possibility of escaping unharmed. But where the odds are completely against him he will quickly withdraw, if possible.

Both the justice of the wilderness and the redeeming chance receive apt treatment in London's "The Men of Forty Mile." Bettles and Lon Mc-Fane get into a quarrel about the existence of "chain-ice" and after exchanging blows decide to have a duel with pistols. Malemute Kid and the rest of their friends are out of all sympathy with the combat. They cannot afford the loss of either man, so they give the combatants the following hopeless alternative: the man that escapes being killed by bullets will be hanged. Since there is no percentage whatever of safety in such a combat, Lon McFane withdraws from it. He makes up his mind that to fight means to give up life whatever happens, even to relinquish the slight chance which favored him in many hazardous ventures of the past.

" 'It's a gloryus game yer runnin', Kid,' cried Lon McFane. 'All the percentage to the house and niver a bit to the man that's buckin'. The

Devil himself'd niver tackle such a cinch—and damned if I do.' "[1]

The point of view of both men is clearly denoted in the following passage:

". . . Both men had led forlorn hopes in their time,—led, with a curse or a jest on their tongues, and in their souls an unswerving faith in the God of Chance. But that merciful deity had been shut out from the present deal. They studied the face of Malemute Kid but they studied as one might the Sphinx. As the quiet minutes passed, a feeling that speech was incumbent on them began to grow. At last the howl of a wolf-dog cracked the silence from the direction of Forty Mile. The weird sound swelled with all the pathos of a breaking heart, then died away in a long-drawn sob."

One of the most characteristic stories of the volume in showing the influence of the North upon the conventional civilized man is "In a Far Country." Its realism is brutal. There is no attempt at suggestion. Every detail is pictured in the morbid life history of two men left alone in a dreary spot to shift for themselves.

Carter Weatherbee and Percy Cuthfert, the former a clerk and the latter a club-man, join an expedition to the Klondike gold fields. They soon become undesirables to the rest of the party on account of their general tendency to shirk and to act selfishly. When the party decides to advance

[1] From "The Men of Forty Mile."

during the winter from their last stop at the Porcu-
pine River, these two men, appalled at the prospect of hardships in traveling determine to remain
at the cabin. The lonesomeness of the North and
the monotony of their mutual companionship, lead
to petty quarrels, to long silences between them,
then to madness and lastly to murder. The psy-
chology of the situation is well interpreted and
the gradual progress from mutual dissatisfaction
and dislike to hatred and insanity are powerfully
recorded.

The effect of the silence on the two men and the
consequent breeding of morbid fears is described
thus:

"To all this was added a new trouble—the Fear
of the North. This Fear was the joint child of
the Great Cold and the Great Silence, and was
born in the darkness of December when the sun
dipped below the southern horizon for good. It
affected them according to their natures. Weatherbee fell prey to the grosser superstitions, and did
his best to resurrect the spirits which slept in the
forgotten graves. It was a fascinating thing, and
in his dreams they came to him from out of the
cold, and snuggled into his blankets, and told him
of their toils and troubles ere they died. He
shrank away from the clammy contact as they
drew closer and twined their frozen limbs about
him, and when they whispered in his ear of things
to come, the cabin rang with his frightened

shrieks. Cuthfert did not understand,—for they no longer spoke,—and when thus awakened he invariably grabbed for his revolver. Then he would sit up in bed shivering nervously with the weapon trained on the unconscious dreamer. Cuthfert deemed the man going mad and so came to fear for his life."[1] The story necessarily comes to a tragic conclusion.

The effect that the North exercised upon London was gloomy in the extreme. In all of his stories there are emphasized over and over again the recall of man to elemental passions, the struggle between life and death and the deadening influence of the white desolation. The grandeur, the solemnity, the somber beauty of the North left their impression along with the horror of its many hardships.

All in all, we are indebted to Jack London for the vivid subjective delineation of a territory that presents Nature in her most moody and most terrible aspects.

[1] From "In a Far Country."

CHAPTER XII

CONCLUSION

LOCALITY AS A FACTOR

IN the previous chapters we have cited many illustrations to show how certain localities impressed the writers of the short story and how the authors utilized the material thus gathered in the practice of their art. It was impossible to be exhaustive. The field of the investigation is too vast to permit it. But we have therefore endeavored to be intensive. Frankly, this has been a task of impressionistic criticism from a set view point: the importance of locality as a contributing factor to the author and his work. The method of treatment was to take a locality, note a few of the men and women who have written short stories about it and of it and endeavor to ascertain just how the locality affected their work. Having done this we are prepared to see why locality has proved so helpful to the development of the American short story and lastly why it has made it the most typically American form of our fiction.

A writer in *The Editor*, which endeavors to be

a magazine of technical interest to authors, says:
"Remember that when once you have placed
your yarn in Kentucky it must *breathe* Kentucky.
Nor are Illinois towns the same as Hoosier towns.
Moral standards vary; church customs vary; trades
and trading vary; a Kentucky "court day" is not
the Northern Saturday; and we may well understand at the outset that the editor expects us,
who strive to reflect the life we know, to be true
and accurate and sensible." [1]

To the short story, locality, therefore, contributes
the *typical* setting. It gives to the short story the
touch of intimacy and reality. It differentiates the
story at once from the mass of other stories, makes
it characteristic and significant. Take New England away from Mrs. Freeman's stories or New
Orleans from Mr. Cable's or the California of '49
from Bret Harte's and we rob them of their greatest charm. In each case mentioned the life of the
locality stamps itself upon the reader, sets up its
own hypotheses, imposes its own conditions and, as
a reward, produces an effect peculiar to itself.

Each locality has a gallery of its own characters. These readily become the principals in a
short story because their crotchets and individual
mannerisms suggest plots. A type like Adoniram
in "The Revolt of Mother" by Mrs. Freeman
presents a problem of forcing a close-fisted, habit-

[1] *The Editor*, January, 1911, p. 5. "The Finer Touches,"
by R. G. Stott.

stunted man into an act of plain duty. Richard
Darrel, the type of the faithful foreman, naturally
shapes a story in which the central motif is self-
abnegation in behalf of his vocation. A character
like "Tennessee's Partner" in the story of that
name by Bret Harte becomes the incarnation of
the *camaraderie* fostered in the rough days of the
Argonauts. Each respective locality furnishes
numerous types of this kind that embody in their
persons the essence of some human trait.

Through characters that are distinctive, plots are
suggested and situations evolved. But in addition
to this source the locality itself, irrespective of its
characters, furnishes interesting and dramatic situations. Thus the loneliness and intense cold of
their Northern camp drive to madness the two
city-bred occupants. The locality, therefore, creates the tragic situation in "In a Far Country."
In one of O. Henry's stories, "Mammon and the
Archer" the entire complication and dénouement are brought about by a typical New York
traffic blockade. The best example of this particular effect is to be found in the work of Hamlin
Garland. Almost every one of the stories in
"Main Travelled Roads" develops through the peculiar nature of the farmer's existence in the Mississippi valley.

Even morality undergoes a change according to
the section where it is to be applied. A sense of
Humanity in the extreme North demands the shoot-

ing of a comrade in distress as we saw in "An Arctic Death" by Jack London. Justice in the West of the golden days was translated to mean the sudden and violent expulsion of all doubtful characters from the limits of the town, e. g., "The Outcasts of Poker Flat." Courage in "The Revolt of Mother" necessitated the defiance of gossip and of a husband's orders. Thus each locality makes its own distinctive appeal to the individual. He acts according to his lights and the prescribed convention of his society. When the two points of view agree we get a typical study. When the individual resists his environment we get a story no less typical but more dramatic.

To summarize, therefore, locality contributes to the short story typical settings, typical characters, typical situations and typical problems of conscience. These, according to the nature of the material, help to produce stories in which the pathos, the tragedy, the comedy and the humor are typical. The old maid in Mrs. Freeman's "A New England Nun" although her point of view and narrowness are universal, nevertheless gains in clearness and in verisimilitude by being depicted as a New Englander. Her entire life in her little restricted provincial community bears out her point of view. The pathos is intensified by being sectional as well as universal because we are dealing with a human being in the concrete and not with an inhabitant of No Man's Land. For other examples of typical

pathos from the stories we have considered may
be cited "Madame Delphine" by Cable where the
problem of the mixture of the races leads to a
pathetic dénouement; "The Star in the Valley"
by Charles Egbert Craddock, where the mountain
girl of rough parentage finds her social status a
bar to love; "The End of the Task" by Bruno
Lessing in which the stifling monotony of the sweatshop creates mental, physical and moral disorders.
In each of the cases cited, as well as in many others
that might be adduced, it is the locality that creates the pathos.

For the typical humor there are stories of plantation negro life by Joel Chandler Harris and Paul
Laurence Dunbar; the whimsical stories of O.
Henry with principal characters drawn from hosts
of metropolitan types; the stories of Bruno Lessing in which the Jewish mannerisms and mental
crotchets evoke a laugh. Much of the work of the
New England short-story writers, somber as it is,
in toto presents humorous individual characterizations as we have already seen.

Even if these were the only contributions that
locality has made to the American short story, they
would be considerable. We have seen in the preceding chapters how powerfully the various settings, local characters, situations, problems of conscience, typical pathos and humor were treated in
the work of some of our greatest short story writ-

ers. There remain, however, a few other inferences to be drawn.

At the time when Dickens, Thackeray, George Eliot and Bulwer Lytton were turning out their most successful work, the United States presented no native authors who ranked with them as novelists in the public esteem. Owing to the custom of serial publication and the vogue of the circulating library, these writers composed long novels elaborated far beyond the practice of to-day. The English periodicals were filled with installments of these works of fiction and also with essays by such men as De Quincey and Leigh Hunt.

For these reasons there was never a great demand for the short story in England. The public did not want it and the writers found it more profitable to produce the three-volume novel and the essay.

The American periodical, however, was forced to resort to native talent and was at a loss for material. Local achievement in the novel was meager. Nor did the American public desire essays. The short story, therefore, sprang up because there was a need for it.

The rapid growth in territorial extent and in population created a corresponding demand for reading matter. The supply of periodicals continued to increase. And as these magazines had to be filled with interesting material, the short story was drafted in to fill the gaps.

In this field our native authors had little or no competition from their English rivals. Dickens, Thackeray, Eliot and Lytton wrote short stories only occasionally and then with a degree of clumsiness and superfluity of detail which made their work inartistic and very much inferior to their novels.

Thus the short story became of necessity a form of fiction produced in America rather than in England. In addition to the periodicals we find in the earlier decades of the nineteenth century a great call for Gift Books and Literary Annuals of all kinds. These were elaborately designed and were filled with sentimental verse and short tales. The moral tale and the "hoax" or "surprise" story were frequently found in their pages. The latter type foreshadowed the technique of the modern story whose interest remains undiminished until the last word is reached.

Thus with a ready and waiting market, the supply was plentiful but the work was still crude both in selection of material and in treatment. When Poe published "Berenice" in 1835 he established a structural standard for all future American work. The unity of impressionism and the use of suspense raised his stories immediately above the efforts of his contemporaries. But a native school of short story writers in spite of Poe and Irving and Hawthorne was not yet firmly founded. They were the pioneers but the great horde of followers was to come a little later.

The first great impulse in that direction came with the appearance of "The Luck of Roaring Camp" in *The Overland Monthly* (1868). Here was a story in which the material was taken from a picturesque American locality and shaped to meet the requirements of Poe's technique. It is said that Harte owed a great deal to Dickens. Perhaps this is so when we remember the English-man's unique powers of vivid characterization and Harte's work in the same direction. But from the structural standpoint Harte's master and the master of them all was Edgar Allan Poe. He did not have the fault of Irving's discursiveness nor of Hawthorne's moralizing. Structurally his work reached perfection, as it is understood to-day.

The sensational success of Harte's work revealed a new source of rich material to the short story writers of our country. The keynote of the future had been struck. In all sections of the United States, as has been shown, there were men and women to follow in Harte's footsteps. With Poe's technique and the rich results of their own ob-servation and experiences they reproduced their localities in all forms of fiction, especially in the short story.

It is clear, thus far, that the unique American market had been created, that canons for successful short-story writing had been expounded by an American and that a distinct impulse to the exploitation of localities had been given by the work of Bret Harte, a Californian. All the forces determining the production of the short story being American, it is not straining a point to call it a typical American product.

But we can go still farther. We can call it the most typically American form of our fiction. The reasons for this are mainly psychological, and peculiar to our country and its localities.

The settling, the cultivation and the development of the immense tract of territory under the stars and stripes have made of us a people feverishly energetic. We are dynamic to a fault. Big cities have sprung up by the tens and immense skyscrapers of commerce by the hundreds. On every hand there is restlessness and change, especially change. Complete neighborhoods are wiped out, to appear in totally strange and new guises. Enterprises on a gigantic scale are constantly being conducted at a vast expenditure of money and nervous energy. Fortunes are still in the making, the social order is not yet fixed. Great hopes dazzle each individual, enticing him into renewed efforts. Unlike the countries of Europe, where everything is rigid, a man's place depending upon his wealth and ancestry rather than on his initiative and energy, here, though the competition is keen, the fighting chance is extended to every man.

The poor farm boy may reasonably aspire to become the president.

Under these conditions there are created numerous ephemeral phases of interest. They concern men, women, industries, occupations, enterprises, politics, economics, religion, art, music,—in fact all that makes our life a journey in which the scenery is ever new from day to day. These fleeting conditions clamor to be recorded. Newspaper statistics show how feverishly active our Press is.[1] Thus we learn that in the United States and Canada there are published twenty-four thousand, two hundred forty-five (24,245) newspapers. The two countries that approach this number nearest are Great Britain with 9,500 and Germany with 8,049. Imagine what a seething cauldron of events this indicates and ask yourself whether the long novel or the short story can best take this transitory life and reproduce its essence. Through its very brevity the short story can take the fleeting emotions of our life, too inconsequential for a complete novel and incorporate them.

Besides the singular adaptability of the short story to record our rapid American progress we have a reading public that, in the main, is unable to concentrate on a long and sustained train of thought. There are thousands of people that read newspapers and periodicals only. This class of readers wants something short, sharp and decisive.

[1] *World Almanac*, 1911, p. 460. Statistics of the Press.

The short story, because of its brevity, because of
its much in little is a favorite form of literature
for minds weary with the day's work and craving
a brief spell of excitement. That is why the adventure story, the story of plot and action rather
than the static or psychological story is in such
demand by current magazines.

The growth of our localities is identical with the
growth of our country, and is therefore responsible
for the development of our short story into what
it is to-day. It is from the constant changes in the
social, political and industrial life of our localities
that the short story derives its greatest impetus.
They furnish the authors with material and create
the fiction hunger which craves for the short story.
It is all a flowing circle of cause and effect invol-
ving the triplicate elements of locality, writer,
reader. The locality spurs on the writer, the
writer furnishes fiction to the reader, the reader
creates the locality.

The short story, therefore, as we have seen,
through the influence of locality and for historical
and psychological reasons may lay claim to being
considered the most typically American form of our
fiction.

BIBLIOGRAPHY

A. CRITICAL, HISTORICAL, BIOGRAPHICAL

ALBRIGHT, EVELYN MAY. The Short Story: Its Principles and Structure. Macmillan.
The Short Story: Technique.
BASKERVILL, WILLIAM MALONE. Joel Chandler Harris. Barbee & Smith, Nashville, Tenn.
Is an appreciation of Harris.
BENNETT, E. A. Fame and Fiction. "Concerning James Lane Allen." E. P. Dutton & Co. 1901.
Contains a critique of James Lane Allen.
BLANC, MME. THÉRÈSE. Questions Americans. Of special interest: "L'Amerique d'autrefois."
Treats the Southern authors from a French standpoint.
BUCKLE, THOMAS HENRY. History of Civilization in England. Vol. 1, Chap. 2.
Shows effect of climate on locality.
CANBY, HENRY SEIDEL. The Short Story: Yale Studies in English. Holt, 1902.
Historical and critical.
CLARK, WARD. Stewart Edward White. *The Bookman,* July, 1910.
Discusses the use of local color in short stories.
COURTNEY, WILLIAM LEONARD. The Feminine Note in Fiction.
Discusses the work of Miss Wilkins.
CUMMINS, MRS. ELLA STERLING. The Story of the Files. Pub. 1893. California: Literary History.

ESENWEIN, J. BERG. Writing the Short Story. Hinds, Noble & Eldredge, 1909.

The Short Story: Technique.

FISKE. Provincial Types in American Fiction. Chautauqua Society.

Treats of the provincial type in the American novel—also touches on the short story.

GILDER, JEANNETTE AND JOSEPH. Authors at Home. Cassel & Co.

Intimate biographical studies of authors in their home environment.

HARKINS, E. F. Little Pilgrimages. L. C. Page & Co. Boston, 1902.

Contains an appreciation of James Lane Allen.

HARTE, BRET. *Cornhill Magazine*, July, 1899.

Bret Harte on his own work.

HAWTHORNE, NATHANIEL. American Note Books. Houghton Mifflin & Co.

Gives the fragmentary hints that were the nucleus of many of Hawthorne's stories.

JESSUP AND CANBY. The Book of the Short Story. D. Appleton & Co.

The Short Story: Historical.

LOCKLEY, FRED. Why They Come Back. *The Editor*, November, 1910.

Illustrates errors made by writers of fiction due to ignorance of locality.

LOVETT, ROBERT MORSS. On Hawthorne's Short Story. *Reader*, August, 1905.

Analysis of Hawthorne's art.

PAGE, THOMAS NELSON. The Old South. Charles Scribner's Sons.

Treats of social conditions in the South before the war.

PAGE, THOMAS NELSON. Social Life in Old Virginia.

Gives a good picture of life in the old South.

POE, EDGAR ALLAN. Review of Hawthorne's Tales. *Graham's Magazine*, 1835.

This article states the underlying principles of short-story technique.

PORTER, SIDNEY (O. HENRY). *Current Literature*, July, 1910.

Autobiographical.

STOTT, ROSCOE GILMORE. "The Finer Touches." *The Editor*, January, 1911.

Contains advice concerning proper use of setting.

WENDELL AND GREENOUGH. History of Literature in America. *Scribner's*, 1904.

A good general history.

1001 PLACES TO SELL MSS. Editor Pub. Co. Ridgewood, N. J., 1912.

Sets forth needs of current magazines in fiction, indicating preferences of setting.

Valuable bibliographies dealing with the following headings can be found in J. Berg Esenwein's "Writing the Short Story," Hinds, Noble & Eldredge:

1. Appendix A: Collections of Short Stories, Sketches and Tales. P. 375.
2. Appendix B: One Hundred Representative Stories. P. 382.
3. Appendix G: (1) Books on the Short Story; (2) Books Referring to the Short Story; (3) Magazine Articles.

B. FICTION

(Arranged according to locality)

BROWN, ALICE. (New England.)
Tiverton Tales. Houghton Mifflin & Co.
Meadow Grass. Houghton Mifflin & Co.

CONNOLLY, JAMES B. (New England Fishing Banks.)
Out of Gloucester. Scribner.

FREEMAN, MARY ELEANOR WILKINS. (New England.)
A Humble Romance. Harper & Bros.
A New England Nun. Harper & Bros.

HAWTHORNE, NATHANIEL. (New England.)
Twice Told Tales. Houghton Mifflin & Co.
Mosses from an Old Manse. Houghton Mifflin & Co.

JEWETT, SARAH ORNE. (New England.)
Tales of New England. Houghton Mifflin & Co.
Strangers and Wayfarers. Houghton Mifflin & Co.

STOWE, HARRIET BEECHER. (New England.)
Oldtown Folks. Houghton Mifflin & Co.
Sam Lawson's Oldtown Fireside Stories. Houghton
Mifflin & Co.

SINGMASTER, ELSIE. (The East: Pennsylvania Germans.)
"Big Thursday." *Century*, Vol. 71, p. 364.
"The County Seat." *Atlantic*, Vol. 101, p. 704.

DEMING, PHILANDER. (New York State.)
Adirondack Stories.

FREDERIC, HAROLD. (New York State.)
The Deserter and Other Stories. Lothrop.

GARLAND, HAMLIN. (The Mississippi Valley, Wisconsin.)
Main Travelled Roads. Stone & Kimball. 1893.

WHITE, EDWARD STEWART. (Michigan, Lumber Section.)
Blazed-Trail Stories. McClure, Phillips & Co. 1904.

COOKE, JOHN ESTEN. (South: General.)
Stories of the Old Dominion. Harper.

DUNBAR, PAUL LAURENCE (colored). (The South: General.)
  In Old Plantation Days. Dodd, Mead & Co. 1903.
SMITH, FRANCIS HOPKINSON. (The South: General.)
  Colonel Carter of Cartersville. Houghton Mifflin & Co.
STUART, RUTH MCENERY. (The South: General.)
  The Golden Wedding and Other Tales. Harper.
JOHNSTON, RICHARD MALCOLM. (Georgia.)
  The Primes and their Neighbors.
WOOLSON, CONSTANCE FENIMORE. (Georgia and Neighboring States.)
  Rodman the Keeper.
ALLEN, JAMES LANE. (The South: Kentucky.)
  A Kentucky Cardinal. *Harper's*, May-June, 1894; Macmillan.
  Flute and Violin. Harper & Bros. 1897.
FOX, JOHN, JR. (The South: Kentucky.)
  Hell fer Sartain and Other Stories. Scribner.
CABLE, GEORGE W. (The South: Louisiana.)
  Old Creole Days. Scribner.
KING, GRACE. (The South: Louisiana.)
  Tales of a Time and Place. Harper.
HARRIS, JOEL CHANDLER. (The South: Middle Georgia.)
  Daddy Jake, the Runaway. Century Co. 1889.
  Tales of the Home Folks in Peace and War. Houghton.
  Nights With Uncle Remus. Houghton.
HARBEN, WILL N. (The South: Northern Georgia.)
  "Two Birds With One Stone." *Century*, Vol. 48, p. 61.
  "The Sale of the Mammoth Western." *Century*, Vol. 53, p. 74.
CRADDOCK, CHARLES EGBERT (MARY NOAILLES MURFREE). (The South: Tennessee.)
  In the Tennessee Mountains. Houghton Mifflin & Co. 1884.
  The Bushwackers. Herbert S. Stone & Co. 1899.

BRADLEY, A. G. (Virginia.)
  Sketches from Old Virginia. Macmillan.
PAGE, THOMAS NELSON. (The South: Virginia.)
  In Ole Virginia. Charles Scribner's Sons. 1892.
ATHERTON, MRS. GERTRUDE FRANKLIN. (The West: Cali-
    fornia.)
  Before the Gringo Came. 1894, also published under
    the title of "The Splendid Idle Forties." Mac-
    millan.
FERNALD, CHESTER BAILEY. (The West: California Chi-
    nese.)
  The Cat and the Cherub. Century.
HARTE, BRET. (The West: California, '49.)
  The Luck of Roaring Camp and Other Sketches.
    Houghton.
  From Sand Hill to Pine. Houghton.
WHITE, EDWARD STEWART. (The West: General.)
  Stories of the Wild Life. McClure, Phillips & Co.
    1904.
THANET, OCTAVE. (The West: Iowa.)
  Stories of a Western Town. Scribner.
PORTER, SIDNEY (O. HENRY). (The West: Texas and
    Adjoining States.)
  Heart of the West. McClure Co. 1907.
GLASS, MONTAGUE. (New York: Cloak and Suit Deal-
    ers.)
  Potash and Perlmutter. Henry Altemus & Co. Phila-
    delphia, 1910.
PORTER, SIDNEY (O. HENRY). (New York City: Compre-
    hensive.)
  The Four Million. Doubleday, Page & Co. 1909.
  The Voice of the City. Doubleday, Page & Co. 1909.
  The Trimmed Lamp. Doubleday, Page & Co. 1909.
  Whirligigs. Doubleday, Page & Co. 1910.
MATTHEWS, BRANDER. (New York City: General.)
  Vignettes of Manhattan. Harper & Bros. 1894.

KELLY, MYRA.   (New York: Jewish School Children.)
  Little Citizens.   McClure, Phillips & Co.   1904.
  Wards of Liberty.   McClure, Phillips & Co.   1904.
LESSING, BRUNO.   (New York: Jewish Life.)
  Children of Men.   McClure, Phillips & Co.   1903.
DAVIS, RICHARD HARDING.   (New York: The Club-man.)
  Van Bibber and Others.   Harper & Bros.   1892.
CRANE, STEPHEN.   (New York: The Slums.)
  Maggie.   D. Appleton & Co.
SULLIVAN, JAMES W.   (New York: The Slums.)
  Tenement Tales of New York.   Holt & Co.
LONDON, JACK.   (Alaska.)
  The Son of the Wolf.   Grosset & Dunlap.   New York.
AUSTIN, WILLIAM.   (Early American work showing traces
     of influences of locality.)
  Peter Rugg, the Missing Man.   New England Galaxy:
     September 10, 1824.

INDEX